A History of

ANDERSONVILLE PRISON

MONUMENTS

A History of

ANDERSONVILLE
PRISON
MONUMENTS

STACY W. REAVES

THE
History
PRESS

Published by The History Press
Charleston, SC 29403
www.historypress.net

First published 2015

Manufactured in the United States

ISBN 978.1.62619.624.7

Library of Congress Control Number: 2015937274

CONTENTS

ACKNOWLEDGEMENTS

O nce again I am humbled and honored to be able to write about one of our great historic sites and national parks. This project would not be possible without the assistance, encouragement and patience of many people. I have been blessed to work with a wonderful library staff at the Southeast Campus of Tulsa Community College, and once again Evelyn Rodgers and the interlibrary loan staff have searched high and low for obscure sources and rare books for this project.

I owe a debt of gratitude to the numerous librarians and archivists at various institutions. I must thank Nan Card at the Rutherford B. Hayes Presidential Library in Ohio for locating sources on the Ohio monument and the staff at the Abraham Lincoln Presidential Library in Springfield, Illinois, for their assistance with records relating to the Illinois monument commission. I must also thank the staffs at the University of Georgia library, the Iowa Historical Society, the Pennsylvania State Archives, the Indiana State Historical Society and the archives at Columbus State University for locating records and photographs.

I cannot forget to thank the National Woman's Relief Corps for its dedication to our veterans and for assisting me with finding information about its work at Andersonville. Two members, Mary Hoover and Jackie Wright, deserve a special thank-you for taking time to share the organization's records, their personal scrapbooks and collected information. They made my visit to Springfield a delight. These women embody the spirit of their past sisters who dedicated their time to caring for our nation's veterans.

ACKNOWLEDGEMENTS

The information on Stalag XVII-B would not have been obtained without the assistance of Bill Doubledee and Doris Livingstone. They provided photos and information about the camp and the ex–prisoner of war association and its work to erect the memorial.

It is so important to make records and archival materials available. I would not have been able to learn as much about artist Bela Lyon Pratt if it were not for the efforts of his family and historical society to publish his records and photos online and to give me permission to use those sources.

I owe a huge thank-you to Janie Lampi once again for attempting to cure her insomnia by proofreading the rough drafts. At this point, she should be starting a list of places to visit on vacation.

This project would not have even begun or gotten very far without the wonderful assistance and encouragement of the staff at Andersonville National Historic Site. I would like to thank Chris Barr and Ava Joiner for sharing their photos of the park. I owe a special thank-you to Hugh Peacock for generously sharing his photography and taking photos for me. Credit for the quality photos belong to these people.

The Friends of Andersonville deserve a special thank-you for providing me with the grant money to travel to Washington, D.C. This provided a large portion of the research and allowed me to share records with the park that the staff had not seen before.

I owe my longtime friend Eric Leonard more than I can repay. He gave me the idea and fed me just enough tantalizing tidbits to hook me on the project. His support, enthusiasm and assistance with research and resources has been invaluable. A special thank-you goes to his wife, Elizabeth Leonard, for opening her home to me during my research trip. I would be remiss if I did not thank the most wonderful host and hostess—Sam and Awyn Leonard. I thank them for being my walking and swimming companions and fellow movie watchers.

Last, I cannot forget my family. My grandparents, Max and Shirley Melton, and my mother-in-law, Alice Reaves, deserve a special thank-you for caring for my girls during my trip to Georgia. Again I cannot repay what I owe or express how grateful I am to my husband, George, and my three daughters—Bessie, Camille and Claire—for their support, patience and enthusiasm. I greatly appreciate my eldest daughter, Bessie, for being my traveling companion to Washington, D.C. Even with all the assistance and support, I am positive there are mistakes and oversights. I take credit for all of them.

INTRODUCTION

I have read in my earlier years about prisoners in the Revolutionary War, and other wars. It sounded noble and heroic to be a prisoner of war, and accounts of their adventures were quite romantic; but the romance has been knocked out of the prisoner of war business, higher than a kite. It's a fraud.
—*John Ransom, Andersonville prisoner*

When taking on this project, I thought I knew the real story of Andersonville Prison. I had read John Ransom's Andersonville diary, and I had seen the historic photos of the prisoners. Thousands of men lived in cramped, filthy quarters with little food and clean water. Thousands died as a result. What more was there to know about the place? As I started researching the history of the site after the war, the real meaning of the place became evident. It was not just a preserved Civil War site with a national cemetery; it was a window into the bitterness that lingered between the North and South after the Civil War. The story of the prison also reflected American's discomfort with the story of military prisoners. Even in the twenty-first century, it is an issue that our county struggles with. The Andersonville story is difficult to process because it is not a foreign enemy torturing our prisoners. It is the story of Americans' treatment of American prisoners.

The prison camp is a blight on Southern history. It does not lend itself to the idea of chivalry, manners and gentlemen. It goes against how Southerners perceive themselves. For Northerners, it was a horror that was to never be forgotten, and someone had to pay for the injustice. The story of Andersonville will continue to divide Americans because it is a story about us in one of our darkest moments. It is easier to accept the brutal treatment of United States prisoners of war by a foreign enemy than by our own people. A foreign nation could not have the same ideas and values as us. Southerners are Americans—how could this have happened?

The story and plight of military prisoners in any war is sorrowful. The punishment and treatment of captives is designed to test their loyalty and strip them of their dignity. Many have said that it is far braver to endure the hardships as a prisoner of war than to face the shot, shell and carnage of battle. After the Civil War, as Americans learned of the wretched conditions of the military prisons, they began to realize that the concept of heroism was not just on a battlefield. Those who lived and died in the prison camps had their loyalty, will to survive and trust in humanity tested. Often, these men felt abandoned by their government but remained loyal to it in order to defy their captors.

By the late nineteenth century, Civil War veterans worried that future generations would not remember the war or the sacrifices of the soldiers. They first began to preserve and memorialize the great battlefields. It was easy to tell the story of men marching to the front, overtaking positions and giving their lives valiantly in battle. It took the silent voice of former military prisoners to point out to the American people that they had fought a battle as well. The ex-prisoners helped the states realize that they must not forget to tell the story of those who were willing to endure incredible hardships and remain loyal to their nation even to death.

The efforts to preserve the prison camp and create the national cemetery tell of the veterans' desire to honor and mourn the prisoners. The story of reconciliation, so often found on the battlefields, does not carry over to prisons and cemeteries. On the battlefields, both armies took losses and bravely fought. At the prison, only one side had to demonstrate their bravery. Union veterans blamed the South for the deaths, often suggesting that it was intentional. They would not forget the atrocities of the prison, nor would they let future Americans forget.

The monuments at Andersonville tell the story of the determination, courage and bravery of the prisoners. Through the memorials erected in the cemetery and prison park, the nation demonstrated its grief over the loss of life and how much the captive men endured. In the cemetery, the figure of Columbia reminds future generations to never forget, and it also lays wreaths on the graves of the fallen brave. Granite soldiers, some haggard and sad, pay their last respects to the men who rest in eternal slumber.

The controversy over Andersonville and the Civil War prisoners will not end. As students and visitors, we can only try to understand the tragedy and hope to prevent it from happening again. As Americans, we can try to honor and remember the men of both sides who fought a silent war within the walls of the prison camps in the North and the South.

DEATH BEFORE DISHONOR

God Help Us! No tongue or pen can describe, or imagination portray,
how horrible is this hell on earth.
—Alfred Voorhees, Andersonville prisoner, June 3, 1864

The men were tired, hot and thirsty. They had traveled several days with stops in various Southern cities awaiting transfer from one prison location to another. Now, ninety Connecticut soldiers shuddered as large wooden doors swung close behind them with a resounding thud. The spectacle in front of them froze their blood. Thousands of walking skeletons with clothes hanging from their frail frames covered in filth and vermin milled about the large enclosure. Makeshift shelters dotted the landscape, and a suffocating smell permeated the whole scene. Several of the men in their unbelief exclaimed, "Can this be hell? God protect us!"

The men had survived and witnessed the horrors of battle numerous times only to find themselves in a different kind of hell on earth. Between February 1864 and September 1865, almost forty thousand Union prisoners witnessed the same scene that the Connecticut soldiers encountered at Andersonville Prison. At the onset of the conflict between the states, both the North and the South thought they would be victorious in a very short period of time. Neither side had considered what to do with prisoners of war, much less how to house and feed them. From the first shots at Manassas and Shiloh, it became clear that the war would not be fought quickly and that both sides would experience losses. Although shocking, both sides could deal with the dead. It was the soldiers captured in battle that became an unending challenge. In the beginning, both sides simply exchanged the captured prisoners. In early 1862, both armies agreed to a formal prisoner-of-war exchange system. By 1863, the Confederates maintained twenty-one military prisons and held more than sixteen thousand in Richmond alone.

Starting in 1863, the Federal army began actively recruiting and engaging black troops in battle. As these African Americans were captured and became prisoners of war, conditions worsened. Politically fighting to maintain slavery, the Confederacy refused to exchange or give equal treatment to these black Union soldiers. In early 1864, troubled by the treatment of African American prisoners of war and the refusal of the Confederacy to recognize them as Federal soldiers, the United States brought a halt to the exchange system. Despite this breakdown, the battles did not stop, and both sides continued to capture enemy troops. The South began failing miserably to provide adequate prisoner facilities and supplies.

The South struggled to find enough food to feed Southern families and its fighting force. Everything from flour to sewing needles had become scarce for Southerners. Despite the hardships faced by the citizens of Richmond, the Confederate government established several military prisons in the city. By 1863, the Union army had moved closer to the Southern capital, and the residents of the city, tiring of the conflict, began complaining to the government about large numbers of Union prisoners held throughout the town. In November 1863, to help resolve the situation, Confederate secretary of war James Seddon ordered Captain William Sydney Winder to find another location for a military prison in Georgia, far away from the front. After an intense search, Winder found land near the small town of Andersonville, Georgia. Consisting of nothing more than seventy poor residents and a train depot, it did have a plot of land just to the east with trees and a stream running through it. Winder determined this site would make an ideal location for a Union military prison. Benjamin Dykes and W.W. Turner, the landowners, seeing an opportunity to make money from the Rebel government, agreed to lease the land to the Confederacy. On January 18, 1864, construction of the prison commenced with much difficulty. Winder had hoped to use local lumber mills for building supplies but found that locals charged exorbitant rates, far too high for the captain's budget. Winder hired a former plantation superintendent to oversee prison construction and used local slaves for labor. Workers cleared timber and used the logs to create a fifteen-foot-high wall with guard towers at intervals of about sixteen feet. Even as the walls were built, prisoners started to arrive. Winder tried to secure food and shelter for the incoming inhabitants, but this proved to be a hopeless task. The captain found himself trapped between locals hoping to make money from the government by supplying the prison and the Confederate leaders in Richmond arguing they had to supply the fighting army instead of Yankee prisoners.

Whether Winder and his men were ready, overcrowded prisons in Richmond and fear of a Union army attack forced the relocation of captives to Andersonville. On February 24, 1864, the first prisoners passed through Andersonville's large double gates. In the middle of the complex, a stream flowed through the stockade. Because the south wall was not yet complete, guards stood watch on the far side of the stream to prevent prisoners from escaping. A Southern surgeon set up white tents inside the walls to serve as a prison hospital. The bedraggled men who entered began collecting wood and creating crude shelters. Some took the few supplied buckets and gathered water for drinking and bathing. Most of the prisoners were relieved to have left the confines of the prisons in Richmond; however, they would soon discover that the place the Confederates called Camp Sumter would not be a relief.

Keeping a watchful eye on the prisoners was of utmost importance. In February, the Fifty-fifth Georgia and the Twenty-sixth Alabama regiments arrived to guard the Federal prisoners. By May 1864, Union forces were making their way through Georgia and Virginia, and the Confederate army needed all fighting units on the front. This forced the Confederate government to move the Fifty-fifth Georgia and Twenty-Six Alabama, thus leaving the prison in need of guards. The Georgia Reserves, made up of old men and young boys not qualified to serve or not wishing to fight, and veterans who could no longer serve on the front replaced the regulars. These men spent their days and nights watching over the thousands of Union soldiers struggling to survive inside the camp. As guards, they enforced the rules, tracked down escapees and, at times, taunted and preyed on the helpless prisoners.

Shelter for the captives became one of the most urgent needs. Captain Winder found that the state and Confederate government could not or would not spare tents to provide housing for the Union prisoners. The wood that was available on the acreage went into the construction of the stockade, the hospital and Confederate shelter and fortifications. Little was left for the federal prisoners. The first captives to enter the stockade quickly snatched up the small pieces of wood lying around and constructed shelters from them. Unfortunately, the majority of the men entering the camp had to figure out shelter using the resources with which they had arrived and what could be found or bartered. Most men used their blankets and overcoats to construct crude personal covers. Those fortunate enough to obtain pine boughs created makeshift wigwams. Others burrowed into the side of the hill. Prisoners quickly learned that some type of shelter was needed or they would become victims of the elements. Charles Hopkins of the First New Jersey Infantry recalled that "starvation, polluted water, exposure to sun and rain, and cold nights and many of them truly sleepless nights, brought on fevers that were almost surely fatal."

Protection from the elements would not be the prisoners' only challenge for survival. Food for both the captives and the guards was precious and scarce. Almost every day, new prisoners arrived at the camp, adding to the number of mouths to feed. Confederate law required that the guards and the prisoners be rationed the same quantity of food. It is unlikely that this was the case at Andersonville. Locals refused to sell produce at the rate set by the Southern government. Poor resource management planning by the Confederate command at Camp Sumter led to small and poor-quality rations distributed to the Union prisoners. The men held in the prison received a quarter of a pound of corn meal or one-third of a pound of bacon. Rice, peas, vinegar or molasses accompanied this. Until the guards completed the cookhouse, the captives had to cook their own meals. Even after finishing the cookhouse, meals were often issued uncooked. Not only was the quantity of food a problem, but the quality was also troublesome. Prisoner Charles Hopkins remembered that the beans came with "cock-roaches and weevil bugs" and that "no effort was ever made to bolt or sieve the corn meal or pick the objectionable substances from the beans or rice." At one point, Captain Henry Wirz, the Confederate commander of the stockade, withheld rations from the emaciated prisoners for three days. Alfred Voorhees, a prisoner, wrote in his diary in response to the withholding of food that he hoped, "the Rebs will all sink in hell before tomorrow morning, this is no place other than a place of starvation." Three days later, Voorhees received a ration of maggoty mush but was glad to receive even this food. Many a stout and robust man would leave the prison as a frail skeleton.

The lack of sanitary water for drinking, cooking and bathing created another obstacle for survival. Winder had selected the site for the prison partially due to the creek that ran through the property. He believed this would provide the Confederate troops and the prisoners plenty of fresh

A map of Confederate Andersonville Prison Camp showing the stockade, the Confederate fort and the town of Andersonville. *Photo courtesy of Library of Congress.*

water. Construction, location of the camp and the overwhelming numbers caused the creek to become a source of illness rather than a source of nutrition. The Rebels constructed their camps and cookhouse upstream of the stockade along the creek. The guards used the water for bathing, cooking, cleaning and sewage. The stream left the Confederate camp and flowed into the stockade where it quickly backed up and no longer flushed out the sinks downstream. The land around the creek quickly became a contaminated swamp. Prisoners learned that drinking water from the stream meant certain death. Using canteens, sticks and makeshift shovels, the captives dug wells for fresh water. In August 1864, heavy rainstorms brought to surface a freshwater spring. The desperate soldiers declared that it was God answering their cries for mercy and later named the water source Providence Springs.

The overcrowding, unsanitary conditions and lack of proper nutrition and shelter caused the death rate to soar. Nearly 29 percent of the prisoners who entered the camp died. Those who lived often suffered from terrible disease and poor health. Soldiers too sick to make it to the sinks often relieved themselves anywhere they could. The filth in the water supply bred disease, and lice and other bugs infested the clothing and bodies of the captives. Prisoner Michael

Dougherty, in misery, wrote in his diary, "The filth and vermin in this place is horrible. Oh, humanity! Oh, Christianity! Where art thou?"

Shortly after constructing the stockade, the Confederate prison command constructed a hospital inside the stockade. It did not last long. Too many sick prisoners overwhelmed the facility. In March 1864, an outbreak of smallpox forced the Rebels to construct another hospital to quarantine the afflicted. The overwhelming numbers also forced them to construct a larger facility outside the stockade. This would also prove inadequate. Every morning, the guards held sick call. The severely ill left the stockade to see doctors and for possible admission to the hospital. If the sick soldier was lucky, he might be placed in a bed. These quickly filled up, and often, the ill found themselves in crowded, ragged tents with little to no bedding on the ground. Between April 25, 1864, and May 9, 1864, doctors treated 1,891 prisoners. Over 300 of those patients died. For every one doctor, there were 200 patients. Not only were physicians in short supply, so were basic medical supplies such as bandages and medicines. This often forced the surgeons to reuse infected bandages, which allowed maggots and gangrene to set in quickly. Prayer was often the best medicine and only hope.

For many, death became their only escape. Those who were not able to make it to the hospital for treatment succumbed to death inside the stockade. One could hope that a friend placed a piece of paper with his identity on his breast so that his name would be recorded. Bodies were carried to the streets or to the gates. Every day, paroled prisoners traveled through the camp with a wagon collecting the bodies. Outside the stockade, the Confederates established a cemetery. Paroled prisoners dug six-foot-wide trenches, placed the bodies side by side and then filled the graves. A wooden board with at least a number marked each grave, and a paroled Union prisoner recorded the names of the dead and grave number.

With many prisoners, discipline and security was of the utmost importance. In March 1864, Captain Henry Wirz assumed command of the inner prison stockade. Prior to being ordered to Andersonville, the Swiss-born captain oversaw all the prisons in the Richmond area. Through his former detail, Wirz had gained experience in managing military prisoner facilities. At Andersonville though, the captain faced numerous challenges. At one point, there were twenty-four thousand Union prisoners and only 1,205 guards. To keep the stockade from being overrun or tunneled underneath by its inhabitants, approximately fifteen feet from the stockade wall, the commander constructed a fence made of a series of posts with horizontal boards across the tops connecting each post. This aptly became known as the deadline. Orders required guards to shoot any prisoner who crossed the line and the horrors of camp life occasionally led crazed men to step across to end their misery. The deadline was not a unique Southern concept. Northern prisons often had the same or a similar feature.

Despite recommendations and requests to stop sending prisoners to the camp, the Confederate government continued to funnel captured Northern soldiers to southwest Georgia. By June 1864, the cramped sixteen acres, designed to hold no more than ten thousand captives, housed more than twenty-four thousand prisoners. To alleviate the crowding, Wirz expanded the prison to twenty-six and a half acres and hoped that the continuous flow of new residents would stop. To gain better control of the prison population and to organize the distribution of rations, Confederates had the men divided into squads of ninety men and then further divided them into messes of thirty prisoners. If a man failed to report to roll call, the guards withheld the food for his squad.

Some prisoners refused to resign to their fate and attempted to escape. One avenue of getting out presented itself during wood details outside the stockade. These escape attempts ended with the guards and hunting dogs returning the prisoner. Afterward, the prisoner could be punished by time in the stocks or a whipping. Details for wood ended as a result. To pass the hours, many prisoners dug tunnels in hopes of fleeing. Using canteen halves, cups, spoons and other makeshift tools, men tried to tunnel under the stockade wall using their shelter or a well as a cover. Some of these ended with the dirt collapsing in on the desperate soldiers. On hearing reports of tunneling attempts, Captain Wirz had the camp searched. The guards discovered one tunnel ninety to one hundred feet long and fourteen feet wide beneath the pickets. Despite the desperate efforts, very few men successfully escaped from Andersonville.

The need for survival led men to steal and become dishonest. Groups of ruthless prisoners began to prey on their fellow captives. The Raiders, as the prisoners called them, took food from the weak and plundered the makeshift shelters for anything valuable or useful. New captives entered the stockade to the cry of "fresh fish" and found themselves surrounded by men who yearned for outside information and others who determined what was worth stealing. To add to the misery of captives, the Raiders not only took whatever they desired but also were rumored to kill fellow captives for a simple possession. Charles Hopkins recalled, "Very often a man was killed outright by some of the raiders just for a little sugar or onions or anything of the type." The terror inflicted by the Raiders incited some of the prisoners to create their own vigilante group. With permission from the prison commander, the Regulators, as they became known, armed themselves and patrolled the inside of the stockade for criminal activity. They arrested almost seventy-five men and found stolen valuables inside the quarters of the accused. To be fair and honest, the prisoners held a trial and found the men guilty. With the approval of Captain Wirz and Richmond, the Raiders were forced to run a gauntlet as their punishment, and six were sentenced to hang. On July 11, 1864, the Confederates constructed a gallows, and the Union prisoners hung Willie Collins, John Sullivan, John Sarsfield, Charles Curtis and Patrick Delany, the ringleaders of the gang. To further add to their dishonor, the burial detail buried the criminals separately from all the other deceased prisoners.

As the Union army advanced into Georgia, Confederate commanders at Andersonville worried about the security of the prison. With the exchange system still halted, the prison population continued to grow. The number of guards did not increase, and the Southerners kept artillery facing the stockade as a threat against mass escape or insurrection. By early September 1864, Union general William T. Sherman's forces began closing in on Atlanta. The prison command decided it was no longer safe to keep prisoners at Andersonville and began moving guards, staff, surgeons and the most able-bodied captives to Florence and Charleston, South Carolina. By mid-November, the prison held a mere 1,500 captives, and Captain Wirz complained that prisoners were regularly escaping due to the poor security available. By December, Union forces threatened Savannah, Georgia. Captives held outside Savannah, many of whom had been at Andersonville, found themselves transferred back to the stockade to survive another winter. By March 1865, the prisoner exchange resumed, and some men began to leave the camp. Confederates, desperate to continue the fight, entered the stockade looking for men who would be willing to join the Rebel fight and escape their misery inside the stockade walls. Despite the feelings of frustration and abandonment, most Yankee prisoners refused to fight against their government. By late March, Wirz began transferring captives to Vicksburg for exchange. In early May 1865, after the surrender of the Confederacy, Union forces entered Andersonville. Federal captain Henry E. Noyes found Wirz and his staff at the camp and placed them under arrest. Young men, withered and emaciated, made their way to their families in the North. Nearly 13,000 men remained in eternal rest at Andersonville, Georgia. The survivors suffered the lingering effects of their captivity, both physically and mentally, for the remainder of their lives.

2

SILENT CITY OF THE DEAD

I have lain on the battlefield in the solemn hours of the night, surrounded with dead and dying and listening to the piteous, agonizing cries of the wounded, but nothing compares to this den of misery and woe, the memory of which will be ever present to those who experienced it.
—*Michael Dougherty, Andersonville prisoner, May 8, 1864*

Chaos seemed to reign over the South at the close of the war. Andersonville was no exception. Federal troops entered the town and prison. They immediately took possession of the stockade and Confederate buildings. The Rebel guards at Andersonville had already begun deserting and heading home before the war had even ended. Captain Henry Wirz, who had lingered behind, found himself shackled and headed toward Washington, D.C., for trial. The locals, taking advantage of the Confederate defeat and abandonment of the site, looted the prison storehouses and began removing lumber. As Union prisoners made the slow return to homes in the North, many found that they no longer resembled the people they were when they left. The time spent at Andersonville left scars on their bodies and minds. They would never forget their time as prisoners of war.

The wooden boards in the cemetery quietly marked the remains of those prisoners who never left Andersonville. Southerners returned to farming and rebuilding their homes and livelihoods. No one wanted to forget the horrors and losses on the battlefields, but no one in the South wished to remember the atrocities at Andersonville. Union commanders in Georgia tried to keep peace and administer loyalty oaths to those Southerners willing to pledge their allegiance to the Union again. Like many Southerners, William A. Griffith traveled through the South, searching for a home and new opportunities. While the train stopped in Andersonville, local African Americans informed him that the graves of the Union dead at the former prisoner site were being washed up. Griffith, appalled by this situation, remained in Andersonville and immediately went to the cemetery. He began to repair those graves that had begun to sink or wash away. In late May 1864, Union general George H. Thomas, commanding Georgia and Tennessee, appointed Griffith the first superintendent of the Andersonville Cemetery. With assistance from local freedmen, the superintendent began constructing a fence around the cemetery and doing general maintenance tasks.

While Griffith cared for the graves in the South, families searched for answers to the whereabouts of loved ones who did not return home. As a result, the cemetery at Andersonville became the center of attention and controversy. Many families turned to the government for answers on the location of their beloved soldiers. The government, overwhelmed with fighting the war and not able to account for every missing soldier, simply didn't give any reply. With great anxiety, many mothers and wives began writing to Clara Barton, who had become famous during the war for organizing medical aid and following the Union army to care for the sick and wounded. In January 1865, Barton's dedication to the care of the men and aiding families led President Abraham Lincoln to appoint her official correspondent for the Friends of Paroled Prisoners. The new appointee spent long days answering anxious inquiries about the location of missing soldiers. Often the broken-hearted woman had to reply that the men had been prisoners of war and their final whereabouts were unknown. The hundreds of letters received almost daily asking for information on the missing soldiers weighed on Barton's heart. The dedicated nurse began to petition Congress to establish an office of missing soldiers and to publish the lists of known Federal dead at confederate prison sites and battlefields. In early April 1865, Barton secured an appointment to meet with the president. The meeting never happened. An assassin's bullet took President Lincoln's life before the appointed date. Barton remained determined and worked to secure the support of Union generals Ulysses S. Grant, Daniel Rucker and Ethan Hitchcock. She contacted Secretary of War Edwin Stanton to arrange for a meeting to discuss establishing an official government Office of Missing Soldiers.

While Barton was working daily to answer questions about missing soldiers, a former private was working to make public the list of dead at

Andersonville Prison. Almost thirteen thousand men lay buried in the cemetery at Andersonville. If a comrade did not send a letter to the loved ones of the deceased, the families had no information regarding their soldiers. Dorrence Atwater held a list that would answer the question for thousands of families. On August 19, 1861, Atwater eagerly enlisted to fight at the young age of sixteen. After obtaining his parents' permission, the Connecticut youth signed up to serve with a cavalry regiment that was later attached to the Second New York Cavalry. On July 7, 1863, Confederate forces captured Atwater in Maryland while he was carrying military dispatches. In February 1864, after surviving five months as a prisoner at Belle Isle, the Rebels sent the young prisoner to Andersonville. Captain Winder, commander of the prison, used Atwater as a hospital clerk; his duties included recording the names of the dead buried there. In February 1865, as the Confederacy collapsed and Atwater transferred to Columbia, South Carolina, with his fellow prisoners, he secreted a copy of the death register and took it with him. In March 1865, after reporting to Camp Parole, Maryland, Atwater wrote to the secretary of war that he had a copy of the Andersonville death register and wished to make the list of names available to the public. After sending the letter, Atwater returned to his hometown in Connecticut to await an answer.

Although the government had an interest in the list of Union dead, it had little desire for Atwater to publish it. In mid-April, the secretary of war responded to the letter and ordered the former private to meet with Colonel Samuel Breck in the adjutant general's office in Washington, D.C. The officer informed Atwater that the government would pay him $300 for the list. In disbelief, the young man refused the money and argued that the names needed to be published for the families of the missing and that he would see this accomplished. Breck warned Atwater that if he published the roll, the army would consider it contraband and confiscate it. Realizing the value to the army and to the American people, Atwater countered with the request of the money and a position as a clerk in the War Department, and in return, he would loan the government the rolls to copy for its records. Agreeing to the deal, Breck took the list of the dead and provided the young man with the money and a position in the War Department.

In June 1865, fully expecting the list of the dead to be returned, Atwater began working as a clerk in the adjutant general's office. After a few weeks, he inquired about the progress of the copying and the return of the list. Colonel Breck gave only vague replies to the young clerk's query and notified the clerk that he would have to contact Secretary Stanton to get the list returned. While Atwater penned a letter explaining his situation and requesting the roll be returned, Breck and the secretary of war discussed the roll, and both concluded that they believed Atwater was hoping to sell the list for profit. Under this assumption, Stanton refused to return the papers.

In disbelief, Atwater turned to another influential person for help in obtaining the names and publishing them. In June 1865, Atwater wrote to Barton explaining his situation and requested her help in obtaining the list and getting it published. Elated that almost thirteen thousand missing soldiers would be identified, Barton went to work on the behalf of Atwater and the families of the deceased. The former nurse discussed the Andersonville list of dead and the plight of the former private with the secretary of war. She also talked with him about the need to mark the graves at the former prison site and establish it as a national cemetery. Stanton, already working to bury Union dead and mark graves elsewhere, agreed with Barton that the government should appropriately mark them and designate the site a national cemetery.

Stanton wasted little time in sending a detail to the former prison camp. In early July 1865, the secretary requested Quartermaster General Montgomery L. Meigs to detail Captain James Moore to travel to Andersonville, Georgia, for the purpose of marking the graves and establishing a national cemetery. In 1861, Captain Moore enlisted with the Nineteenth Pennsylvania and, two years later, transferred to the quartermaster's department. In July 1864, due to the large number of graves scattered across the South, the United States Congress created a special unit for graves registration, and Moore found himself detailed to this new unit. Almost a year later, the quartermaster general sent Moore to the Spotsylvania and Wilderness battlefield for the purpose of giving the Union dead a proper burial. On June 30, 1865, as the captain and his detail finished the gruesome task, he received orders to go to the Andersonville Prison site and to take Dorrence Atwater and Clara Barton with him.

The captain prepared to leave for Georgia immediately by gathering the needed supplies and informing Barton and Atwater to prepare to leave Washington. On July 8, Barton and Moore's expedition found that the trip to Savannah, Georgia, was a problem. The conditions of roads and trains in the South made travel within Georgia slow and difficult. On arrival in Savannah, the captain discovered that there was no railroad line to Andersonville, and the direct line to Macon was down, as well as the one to Augusta via Atlanta. Deciding that travel by road would be an alternative, Moore tried to procure wagons for his equipment and men. The general commanding the department informed him that there simply were not enough horses or mule teams available in the state to pull the wagons needed. The general also informed him that the roads across the state were in poor repair, and travel would be difficult. After a week contemplating his alternatives, Captain Moore decided to procure a boat and travel along the Savannah River to Augusta.

Determined to complete his mission, Moore and the expedition arrived in Augusta, Georgia, on July 19, 1865. By this time, the railroad to Macon was running, and the group took the train to Macon and from there to Andersonville. Moore assigned Barton to a car on the train, but the woman found that despite her desire to see the graves properly marked and to answer the letters of concerned families, the captain did not welcome her presence. The officer tolerated her, but did not go out of his way to give her special accommodation beyond what was required of her gender. Barton found this to be troublesome. One evening shortly after beginning their train trip, Barton realized that the captain had eaten dinner but had not invited her to eat with him or the other members of the expedition. Moore found the woman and her fame, which drew visitors, to be a nuisance, and he wondered aloud why she even wanted to make such a trip.

Captain Moore's expedition arrived in Andersonville on July 26, 1865, and found much evidence of the horrors of the camp still in existence. The cemetery, as Atwater and others described, remained. Griffith, who had arrived shortly after the end of the war, had started building a fence around the graves. The stockade walls, wells and many of the Confederate buildings stood abandoned as eerie reminders of the unspeakable conditions. While in Macon, Moore detailed the 137th United States Colored Troops and the 4th U.S. Cavalry as laborers for his mission. The army expedition, using Atwater's list and the rolls confiscated from the Confederate hospital, began working to create new markers and identify the names of each man in the long massive graves. Barton, who set up her own tent on the grounds, answered the many letters of inquiry as she learned the names. The Northern lady became a curiosity to the local freedmen. The former slaves inquired as to the validity of the rumors that they were indeed free and that President Lincoln was dead. Barton read the orders explaining they were to be paid for their labor and what constituted a workweek. She also verified that the president, who had signed their freedom, was dead. The local Southern women visited Barton as well. The women discussed the terrible treatment of the Northern prisoners and the tragedy that occurred there. Despite the efforts of the local women to sound sympathetic, the Northerner found it disconcerting that a few of the women exonerated Captain Wirz, who was awaiting trial for war crimes in Washington, arguing that treatment of the prisoners was the work of General Winder and other Confederate commanders.

Barton tried to stay out of Moore's way and assist the local freedmen. Unfortunately, Moore found himself needing the assistance of the former nurse. The intense Georgia heat and humidity bred typhoid fever and several of the laborers became ill. Barton, no stranger to caring for the sick, quickly went to work caring for the men. Only one man died, and Moore returned his body to his family.

The captain and his expedition had completed the task of setting up the cemetery by mid-August. The bodies were laid in rows only twelve inches apart. As a result, the wooden headboards almost touched one another. About 120,000 feet of pine became the first permanent markers for the Andersonville dead. Moore completed the fence that Griffith had started and created one large avenue through the center of the cemetery and then subdivided it into blocks. In anticipation of the place needing a permanent caretaker, the officer constructed his own quarters to remain as housing. On August 17, 1865, Captain Moore, gathering his crew and the newspaper reporters, asked Clara Barton to raise the flag in the newly created cemetery at Andersonville. Barton recalled that the flag went up the pole, "and there it drooped as if in grief and sadness, until at length the sunlight streamed out and its beautiful fold filled." At the site of the flag, the compassionate Barton covered her face and wept. Due to the records kept by the Confederates and the list provided by Dorrence Atwater, of the 12,912 graves marked, only 451 were unknown.

For Atwater, the return to Washington, D.C., was not the end of his troubles or the controversy over the list of dead. Immediately on returning, Captain Moore wrote to Colonel Breck informing him that list had been removed from his tent by Atwater, and the clerk refused to return it unless he received remuneration. Breck had the former prisoner of war arrested under the charges of conduct prejudicial to good order and military discipline and larceny. The general court-martial hearing found Atwater guilty, fined him $300 and sentenced him to hard labor for eighteen months. The other stipulation of his sentencing was that the clerk was to return the list to the War Department. Until the register was returned and the money was paid, Atwater would remain at hard labor. Outraged, Clara Barton went to work securing the clerk's release and clearing his name. In February 1866, with the assistance of Barton, Atwater had the list published in the *New York Tribune*. On November 30, 1865, President Andrew Johnson pardoned

Atwater. Unfortunately, the dishonorable discharge and reputation as a thief remained. Atwater, Barton and several congressmen worked for years introducing bills to clear Atwater's name and to set up a congressional committee to investigate the charges against him and his treatment by the War Department. Finally, on March 23, 1898, a special act of Congress absolved Atwater of all charges and annulled his dishonorable discharge from the army. By this time, the former prisoner of war had become disillusioned with his government and the war department and had left the country.

Captain Moore's desire to keep the list of dead for the War Department may have come from good intentions. Moore, already familiar with establishing cemeteries, began working with the War Department to publish lists of the dead buried in the South and military posts in the west. Before 1865, the government published two volumes of the series *Roll of Honor*. It was the goal of the War Department to publish the names of those at Andersonville and Spotsylvania in a third volume. On submission of Moore's report of the expedition, the request was made to the secretary of war to publish the names, noting, "The lists are much sought after by officers of the states and public societies and libraries." This was the reason behind the desire to copy Atwater's list and perhaps to keep the names from being published by a private entity.

A view of Andersonville National Cemetery, circa 1906. *Photo taken from* Report of the Unveiling and Dedication of Indiana Monument at Andersonville, Georgia.

Cemetery headstones in Andersonville National Cemetery. Notice how closely the stones are positioned. This reflects how close burial crews buried the dead.

Andersonville became one of many national cemeteries created during this period. After battles, the armies buried the dead. Union army troops often buried their men in trenches or in one location on the battlefield, thus creating a cemetery for their deceased. This was on private property, and there were no guarantees that the graves would be maintained or even officially marked. In July 1863, President Lincoln signed an act allowing the government to purchase the cemetery grounds where soldiers who died in service to their country were buried. By 1864, the government reburied and marked the graves at twenty-seven sites and designated them national cemeteries. The sites would receive constant oversight and upkeep by the government, and only those who honorably served their country could receive burial there. In August 1864, Andersonville became one of the official resting places for Federal soldiers. By 1870, the department had designated seventy-three sites as national cemeteries.

3
A CONQUERED LAND

No name, no regiment to tell what state has missed a star from its crown of glory. We call those graves unknown, but God has their names on His roll-call; for He gives His angels charge of those that sleep; while He Himself watches with those that wake.
—Rhode Island state monument dedication

The huge, imposing wooden stockade wall stood silently around the twenty-six acres. Inside it, holes dotted the landscape, and half-dug pits covered the slopes. Food refuse, debris and waste clung to the grass and mud surrounding the creek running through the pen. Spoons, buckets and plates lay abandoned on the ground. Outside the walls, the fort, the cabins and the earthworks continued to watch over the prison grounds. Instead of hundreds of human voices filling the air, only the sound of birds singing and the wind gently blowing could be heard. These were the physical remains of Andersonville Prison. It was a testimony to the horror and wretchedness of the Confederate prison.

The Union army occupied the South after the war and took control over the confederate prison site. W.A. Griffith, receiving the first appointment as the cemetery superintendent, worked to preserve the remains. As the United States War Department prepared to court-martial Henry Wirz and debated the culpability of Jefferson Davis and other high Confederate leaders, the remains of the prison provided physical proof of the cruelty. Locals in the Andersonville area attempted to rebuild their lives and move past the war. The site of the national cemetery and the prison stockade had belonged to

Benjamin Dykes and W.W. Turner prior to the rebellion, and the federal government, after capturing the site, continued to hold claim to it. In the late spring of 1865, Dykes decided to reclaim his property. Superintendent Griffith informed the landowner that he could not take possession of any of the buildings nor remove anything from the place. Angry, the Southern landowner informed the superintendent that he was the legal owner of the land and had been since 1857. Griffith informed Dykes that as a citizen he could submit his title and claim to the government, but as the federal agent of the site, Griffith had no authority to allow him to reclaim the property. Furthermore, the superintendent informed the landowner that if he entered the premises again, it would be considered trespassing.

Returning to his family in Andersonville, Dykes pondered the situation with his land and the federal government. Prior to the war, he had farmed the site, but during the war, the Confederates had erected numerous structures, including the stockade, and increased the value of the land. Unfortunately, they had also buried thirteen thousand bodies in it. Realizing the importance of the cemetery to the government and its uselessness to him, Dykes offered to give the government the fifty acres comprising the national cemetery if it would release the claim on the rest of the land. He further added that if a fair price could be reached, he would be willing to sell the rest of the land to the government. A few days later, Griffith and Dykes met to discuss the price. After talking with his superiors, Griffith believed that the government needed more than the fifty acres. The landowner offered the government agent 990 acres for $8,000. This was too high, and the two seemed unable to agree on a price. Both men decided to have the land appraised. A few weeks later, the men agreed on $5,000, and Griffith informed Dykes that he would forward the paperwork to Washington, D.C. After waiting months to complete the agreement, the frustrated landowner learned that the papers were never forwarded, and he still could not take possession of the land. In desperation, Dykes wrote to the quartermaster general and Captain James Moore explaining his situation and complaining about the superintendent. The Southerner reported the confiscation of his land and demanded rent or damages or that the property be returned. Trying to get sympathy, Dykes also claimed that he was a crippled noncombatant Southern citizen who had taken his loyalty oath.

The Andersonville site presented a quandary. It had been the scene of terrible suffering for Union soldiers and was the final resting place for several thousand. Trying to get an understanding of the situation at the former prison and the legitimacy of Dykes's claims, the quartermaster general asked Captain Moore about the claimant. Moore answered that he knew very little about the Southerner other than he had been pointed out to him during the expedition as the landowner. Having seen and heard of the horrid treatment of Union captives and a growing hatred of Southerners, Moore reasoned that the land should not be given back to Dykes because the timber making up the stockade would be a valuable windfall for him. Claiming to learn that Dykes had proposed to build a vineyard on the cemetery grounds, Moore told the general that the Southerner was a violent man and an enemy of the government. Taking the captain's comments into consideration, the quartermaster agreed not to relinquish the land to Dykes but to secure the cemetery, the stockade and the adjacent lands for the purpose of preservation. In February 1866, Dykes wrote to the secretary of war requesting the return of his land and tenants. Further, the Southerner noted that he had received his pardon and would like to request the appointment of superintendent of the cemetery at Andersonville. Secretary Stanton pigeonholed the letter and did not reply. Already, Northerners realized that this was a sacred place that should be preserved to honor those who had suffered there.

By the end of January 1866, it appeared the government would not return the land to a white Southern property owner. People were recommending that the government take permanent possession of the site. In February 1866, Charles H. Howard—brother of General Oliver O. Howard, the head of the Freedmen's Bureau—wrote to Republican congressman Henry Wilson recommending that the government take ownership of the site. Howard noted that the site was not only one of great meaning to the families of those left in graves but also to those who survived. Bitter feelings ran high among Northerners over the atrocity, and Southerners believed that they were wrongly blamed for the prison. In the letter, Howard noted that attempts had already been made to destroy the stockade and the buildings, leaving no evidence or useable property for the freedmen.

Conflict and changing superintendents further added to the confusion and troubles for those Southerners trying to the reclaim their land. Due to his interest in the site and work caring for the graves, Major General Thomas conferred the appointment of superintendent to W.A. Griffith, and Captain Moore agreed with the appointment. By the fall of 1865, the quartermaster general received complaints about Griffith. One charged that he was a former Rebel officer, and H.B. Wilton sent a letter charging that the caretaker was selling commissary stores and whiskey from his quarters at the national cemetery. To further add to the case against the superintendent, Benjamin Dykes continued to complain about him. Dykes wrote asking for the government to force Griffith to pay him rent or damages. The Southerner reported that the caretaker destroyed the lumber on the land and sold the bricks for profit and had also sold or bartered other items from the prison site. On November 20, 1865, the district commander relieved Griffith and appointed H.B. Wilton as superintendent of the Andersonville Cemetery.

With money and jobs scarce in the South, the superintendent position of the cemetery presented itself as a comfortable job that many sought. After Wilton's appointment, the quartermaster general requested more information on both men from Captain Moore. The captain reported that he believed that Griffith was indeed a capable Union man and argued that Wilton lied about Griffith to get the superintendent position. Moore further added that Wilton was misinformed about the former superintendent being a former Rebel. Griffith was a loyalist who received persecution during the war and had cared for the remains at his own expense before receiving the appointment. Moore reasoned that Wilton schemed to get the position out of malice and pointed out that last July, Wilton, having no money and "in very indigent circumstances," was employed to draft a map of the prison pen and its surrounding area. Wilton had represented himself as an excellent draftsman and yet after two months failed to produce any drawings. Afterward, Moore ordered the man's discharge, and Wilton then subsisted on the charity of Griffith for several weeks. After some deliberation and investigation, Meigs dismissed Wilton and reappointed Griffith.

In March 1866, General James Wilson, military occupation commander of Georgia, visited Washington and called on Meigs to report that his own investigation at Andersonville revealed that Griffith or his brother had served the Confederacy and now had taken over Andersonville. Wilson further reported that visitors to the cemetery were shocked and offended to find a Rebel overseeing the cemetery. The general recommended Wilton as superintendent and pointed out that the man had been a prisoner of war at the prison and was a Union man from Atlanta. A month later, the quartermaster general received yet another letter. This time, it was a forwarded letter from C.M. Plumb to Major General Ethan Allan Hitchcock, commissioner of exchanges, arguing that appointing Griffith superintendent of the Andersonville cemetery was a huge mistake. Plumb recounted Griffith's dismissal in November and added, "Griffith is an ignorant, coarse, drinking, swearing and disloyal fellow." The writer accused the superintendent of cheating his laborers, speaking of the dead at Andersonville as wash and saying that the loyalty oath was of no account. With vehemence, Plumb told the major general that Griffith's appointment was "an insult to all who have friends at Andersonville, not only, but to the entire North." The man suggested that Wilton be appointed, noting that he was a persecuted Southern Union man who was honest and of proper intelligence. Plumb further added that he had met both men on a visit to the cemetery and that the quartermaster general needed to investigate Griffith's appointment and Captain Moore, who established the cemetery. The writer suggested that Moore was guilty of offenses worthy of the penitentiary in reference to Clara Barton and Dorrence Atwater. About the same time that Meigs received Plumb's letter, he also received a letter of complaint against Griffith from Massachusetts senator Henry Wilson. The senator echoed many of the same charges against the superintendent and advocated Wilton's appointment.

Meigs, confused and frustrated with the situation in Georgia, called on Captain Moore for an opinion once again. The captain responded that his opinion of both men had not changed, but he believed that Griffith would continue to be a target for potential rivals and recommended that the general appoint a "high toned discharged officer or soldier" to the position. Meigs contemplated the matter. The position seemed to be one of great interest to numerous people, and he had received two letters from former prisoners of the camp requesting to be appointed. That spring, the general appointed a neutral person, C.A. Van Deuerson, the nephew of former New Jersey governor William A. Newell.

Wilton refused to give up on the superintendent position at Andersonville, and in July 1866, he wrote to the head of the Georgia Division that the Confederates were attempting to take over the Andersonville site. Wilton charged the new superintendent of being addicted to whiskey and unable to perform his duties. The disgruntled former superintendent claimed that those working against the government took advantage of Van Deuerson's addiction to gain jobs and positions of influence and trust at the cemetery. The letter prompted yet another investigation of the cemetery management. The acting assistant inspector general for the Department of the South, Captain S.C. Greene, headed this investigation and visited the site personally, where he found everything in order. The six-foot picket fence surrounding the cemetery was freshly whitewashed, and a firebreak had been created between the fence and forest. The seven freedmen and three former Confederates who labored under Van Deuerson had also erected three gates. Greene spent time interviewing locals and the workers about the superintendent's habits and character. After returning to his headquarters, Greene reported back that he could find no evidence to corroborate the charges against Van Deuerson. Meigs ignored the letter of complaint and allowed his new appointee to continue his work.

Reconstruction politics and policies regarding the newly freed slaves created tension between the government and the Southern landowners. In early 1865, the federal government created the Freedmen's Bureau, also known as the Bureau of Refugees, Freemen and Abandoned Land. This bureau helped distribute food rations, build schools and resettle freedmen on abandoned and confiscated lands in the South. In January 1866, the cemetery superintendent began hiring local freedmen to work in the national cemetery. Most of these workers lacked not only jobs but also housing. As the prison site still had the numerous buildings constructed by the Confederates and several acres of open land, Superintendent Van Deuerson allowed local freedmen and his laborers to move into the empty buildings or to erect their own houses on parts of the former prison. Former slave and cemetery employee Albert Williams moved into the building used as a smallpox hospital during the war and cleared the land to plant crops for his family.

Under President Andrew Johnson's Reconstruction policies, violence in the South against the former slaves escalated. Hate groups such as the Ku Klux Klan developed, and the area around Andersonville experienced the same problems, chaos and hostilities as many other parts of the South.

A view of the stockade grounds in the late nineteenth century. *Photo taken from* Pennsylvania at Andersonville, Georgia: Ceremonies at the Dedication of the Memorial.

Earlier, in 1860, the American Missionary Society established a school for the free blacks in Sumter County, Georgia. Under the Freedmen's Bureau, the missionaries returned and reestablished the school in one of the prison buildings, and the cemetery laborers and other freedmen in the area attended it. The resettlement of the former slaves and continued control of the prison site by the military only added to the existing hostilities. Benjamin Dykes continued to petition to reclaim his land, and when it became obvious that the government had no intention of relinquishing control, he took matters into his own hands. In 1868, Dykes went to the homes of the freedmen living on his former property and told them to vacate the premises within four days or he would have the sheriff evict them. With the short notice, the tenants had nowhere to go nor any idea of what to do. Several asked to rent the land from Dykes, but he refused. On July 29, 1868, Dykes returned with a large group of armed white men. The men entered the homes and threw out all the freedmen's belongings, nailed the doors shut and exited the houses by making a hole in the roof. A group of curious whites gathered outside to watch. Adding to the freedmen's humiliation, a thunderstorm burst through the clouds and rained down on them.

Dykes was not the only person claiming title to prison property. A Mr. Crawford reported that he owned the land on the south end of the stockade. That summer, Crawford called on Albert Williams and several others living around the property and demanded rent and to sign a contract agreeing to sharecropping. When the tenants could not pay the percentage, Crawford, Dykes and a representative for Crawford raided the properties, taking corn, sows and hogs. Local whites, possibly the Ku Klux Klan, also made attempts to burn down the stockade and buildings. Reverend Pierson Hamilton, a missionary in the area assisting the former slaves, tried to help the freedmen find justice but to no avail. One night, the minister received a letter from the local Klan accusing him of being a meddling copperhead and threatening his life if he did not leave within twenty-four hours. Hamilton promptly left the next morning and later gave a report to Congress on the conditions of freedmen in Georgia.

Benjamin Dykes and the other white men's violence against the freedmen did not help their case to reclaim the land. In February 1870, the Military District of Georgia issued orders forbidding Dykes on the property at Andersonville and ordered the superintendent to consider it trespassing if the Southerner entered the grounds. The orders were to stand until a federal court could issue a decree on the property. In September 1875, Dykes's legal case against the government made its way to the federal court. The former landowner continued to claim that the Confederates never paid him for use of the land and the federal government took it and cleared the timber and bricks from it. He asked the courts to award him $65,848.50. The courts ruled against it. In February 1875, realizing that he would never recoup the land or the loss of money from the timber, Dykes sold the land to the government, and the government purchased the rest of the land from W.W. Turner's heirs.

By the mid-1880s, veterans began returning to the battlefields they had once fought over. Some returned to southwest Georgia to see the site of their captivity. This was a site that continued to haunt their memories more than their battlefield experiences. The imposing stockade wall was mostly gone. Some of the logs rotted away, and locals and visitors removed the wood for souvenirs. Weeds had grown up in part of the land around the stockade, and farmers planted in the other parts. Although the federal government maintained and improved the national cemetery, veterans found it disturbing that stockade site was not being maintained as a memorial to those who had died and the survivors. Earlier visiting military personal recommended the preservation of the site as a memorial. In 1868, First Lieutenant A.W. Corliss went to Andersonville to complete work at the national cemetery and recommended that the government preserve the prison site as a national memorial. Corliss argued that it would not take much effort to care for the structures and preserve them as they had been during the war. The army did not respond. Shortly after Corliss's recommendation, Adjutant General Lorenzo Thomas visited the site on business. Lorenzo informed the cemetery superintendent that the stockade should be preserved. The cemetery superintendent wrote to General Meigs asking for more laborers to adequately preserve the stockade wood that was decaying and further pointed out that the government did not have the deed to the land. Meigs did not have the money in his budget to preserve the site, and he believed Congress was not ready to allocate funds for such a task. If the site were to be maintained as a memorial or shrine, it would be the responsibility of the veterans to preserve it.

By the end of the war, before the military mustered out all the men, the soldiers began planning reunions. By late May 1865, the Third Army Corps and the Army of the Tennessee formed, and in the months that followed, several other veteran groups organized. The men created the organizations as a way to reunite and reminiscence with their former comrades in arms, support political leaders who worked for the veterans and to provide protection and advancement of the former soldiers. In March

1866, Dr. William Stephenson and his wartime comrade W.J. Rutledge met in Springfield, Illinois. The two men had both served with the Fourteenth Illinois Infantry during the war and had made plans before the war ended to create a brotherhood organization for veterans. The next month, after meeting with a large number of Illinois veterans, the two men formed the first chapter of the Grand Army of the Republic in Decatur, Illinois. The organization, which worked to secure care and education for orphans of deceased soldiers, pensions for widows and orphans and to provide homes for the homeless veterans, quickly grew in numbers. By 1890, it boasted a membership of almost 500,000 former Union soldiers. It only seemed natural that these veterans would have an interest in honoring those who suffered at the hands of the Confederates in Andersonville. In the spring of 1891, the Georgia department of the Grand Army of the Republic purchased seventy-three and a half acres that included the entire stockade except part of the northwest corner, fortifications and a right-of-way leading toward the train depot.

The veterans put great care into the cleaning and maintenance of the prison site. Restoring and clearing the ground of the recently constructed buildings was the first order of business. Although the stockade walls were gone, there was still evidence of the prison pen. The wells, desperately dug by the prisoners, still dotted the landscape where the men once lived. These had to be preserved for future generations as a testimony to the brutal conditions in which the prisoners had survived. The GAR planted hedges around the wells in an effort to preserve them and constructed three bridges on the site, thus allowing buggies and carriages to tour the site more easily. With great respect, the old soldiers worked tirelessly to restore the land and maintain it, but despite their best efforts, they discovered that the task of caring for it required money. The veterans' fundraising efforts to pay off the mortgage and to provide money for upkeep began to fall short. In 1897, the Grand Army of the Republic approached the Woman's Relief Corps (WRC) about becoming the new caretakers.

At the 1897 annual meeting, the WRC gave the offer serious consideration. The WRC was the largest official ladies auxiliary to the GAR. After the war, wives, sisters and mothers also began forming veteran aid societies with the purpose of perpetuating the memory of the men's valor and to help with social conditions faced by the veterans and their families. The forerunners of the Woman's Relief Corps started as a ladies aid society in Massachusetts and Ohio in the late 1870s. Over time, women in other Northern states organized other chapters and societies. In 1881, at the annual encampment of the Grand Army of the Republic in Denver, Colorado, the veterans passed a resolution creating the National Woman's Relief Corps as an official women's auxiliary to the organization. However, the resolution did not take effect until 1883, when GAR commander in chief Paul Van der Voort made the resolution effective and thus combined the various state organizations into one. The veterans recognized and helped organize the women with the idea that they would assist the Grand Army of the Republic with its mission of perpetuating the memory of the dead and aiding veterans and their widows and orphans. Even though most of the members were female relatives of Civil War veterans, membership was not limited to relatives. Any loyal woman who believed in the society's mission and was of good moral character could join. By 1885, the corps had grown to twenty-two departments, three provisional departments and 20,226 members.

At the 1897 annual meeting, the WRC considered the offer and passed a resolution accepting the twenty-five acres of the Andersonville Prison site that included the land used as the stockade. This would be given to the Woman's Relief Corps free of debt under the condition that the women would improve the property and keep the grounds in order and "forever hold it as a sacred memory of the heroic loyal men who suffered imprisonment there." The resolution passed unanimously, and the women accepted the agreement. To facilitate upholding the agreement, the WRC created a board of trustees to take charge of the property, and to raise funds for the improvements and maintenance, the national convention asked each corps to contribute five cents per member to the Andersonville fund. The money could be raised through personal contributions or any manner that the corps decided on. The women agreed that it was a small sum, but "would help…care for the Andersonville prison property, the place made sacred by the suffering and agony of starvation and thirst of our Union soldiers confined there."

The WRC immediately established a board of trustees to manage the site. Fellow corps members elected seven women to the board and requested that the commander in chief of the Sons of Union Veterans serve as an ex-officio member of the board. To oversee daily operations of the site, the women decided to elect Lizabeth Turner of Boston to serve as the manager. Turner, born in East Windsor, Connecticut, on February 1, 1829, married Francis F.L. Turner, a Georgia native. The couple spent most of their marriage in his native state. Turner's husband died in 1853, and she returned to New England and become involved in business. With her husband dead, Lizabeth Turner had no relatives serve in the war, but she did her part by caring for the sick and wounded at a hospital in Boston. Like many of the Northern women, the widow also sent care packages to the Union soldiers serving on the front lines. In March 1880, Turner joined the WRC chapter in Malden, Massachusetts, where she served as the treasurer and president. After the Grand Army offered the property to the WRC, Turner accompanied a group of members to inspect the property, and she helped adopt the resolution to accept it. To serve as the property manager and caretaker of the sacred site would be an honor to which she would dedicate the remaining years of her life. On April 27, 1907, while visiting Andersonville, Turner passed away. She had given her whole heart to honoring and perpetuating the memory of those who suffered in the prison. Veterans who visited would never forget the warm, sincere and caring welcome they received from Turner when they visited the site.

The women of the WRC vowed to protect the "wells they [prisoners] tried to dig with their naked hands…and the spring the Lord opened with a thunderbolt in answer to their dying prayers." Lizabeth Turner and the board of trustees immediately placed a wire fence around the property to mark the boundaries and iron gates to allow visitors entrance. They added culverts and bridges over the small creek that ran through the grounds to prevent washouts, built a road around the entire park for ease of viewing for the old veterans and erected a flagstaff and an archway over the entrance. Where visible reminders of the location of the stockade wall, the deadline and the desperately built wells remained, the WRC erected small wooden signs for visitors. Realizing that veterans and families making pilgrimages to the park would need a comfortable place to stay and gather, the women erected a nine-room house that various state corps furnished. They also added a tool shed and a barn. Although the members donated money for the upkeep of the grounds and the house, additional funding sources were needed. Lizabeth Turner planted two hundred pecan trees on the ground with hopes that the sale of the pecans would make the park self-supporting. Last, with an eye toward beauty and peace, Turner planted thirty rose bushes outside the cottage. In 1897, realizing that they did not own the entire prison pen, the WRC purchased the remaining fourteen and a half acres from the landowners. Now the women owned the majority of the prison, fort and earthworks that composed the Andersonville prison.

Between 1897 and 1910, the WRC improved and preserved the grounds of the prison. As part of their mission, they worked to perpetuate and honor the memory of those Union soldiers who suffered and died for their country at the horrible place. In 1868, General John A. Logan, a member of the Grand Army of the Republic, proposed the observance of Memorial Day. The Woman's Relief Corps took it upon itself to properly observe this day every year, and after the corps acquisition of the Andersonville site, Turner hosted Memorial Day observances in which local freedmen and veterans gathered in the national cemetery to decorate the graves with flags and roses from the cottage garden. The WRC caretaker hosted visiting state commissions and delegations who visited to select memorial sites and during the dedication ceremonies. Not only did the WRC encourage and support the construction of memorials at the park, but it also erected several memorials of its own, including one to Lizabeth Turner in honor of her hard work and dedication. In 1901, working with the Ex–Union Prisoners of War Association, the women erected a pavilion over the spring. In 1907, at the sixteenth convention, the women appointed a special committee to investigate transferring the site to the government. Despite the corps' best efforts, the cost of maintaining the site was proving to be too costly and hard to manage without a dedicated member on site.

The United States Army seemed the logical choice for taking over the preservation of the site. By 1900, the secretary of war and the Quartermaster Department preserved and maintained four Civil War battlefield sites: Shiloh, Vicksburg, Chickamauga and Antietam. The government had maintained and supervised the national cemetery at Andersonville since its creation in 1865 but had no control or jurisdiction over the prison and the Confederate fort and fortifications. After the Grand Army of the Republic and the Woman's Relief Corps purchased the property containing the prison and the Confederate fort, the army still had no control or say over the use of the land.

In 1908, the WRC began approaching the army about taking over the site to ensure its future preservation. On March 2, 1910, by an act of Congress, the secretary of war authorized the army to accept the eighty-eight acres as a gift from the Woman's Relief Corps and the Grand Army of the Republic. The quartermaster department now maintained the national cemetery and the entire prison site. The WRC cottage and outbuildings transferred to the army with the understanding that the Woman's Relief Corps would continue to furnish the cottage so that visiting veterans might use the facility. While accepting the transfer bill, Michigan senator James A. Foraker asked that the name be changed to Andersonville Prison Park. After accepting the change, the quartermaster general sent orders to the cemetery superintendent that the prison was to be left undisturbed except for work deemed necessary, such as upkeep of the lawn, roads, walks and enclosure. As the general stated, "In other words it is not the desire to disturb the present arrangement of any of the flower beds, walks, enclosure, monuments, wells, streams or buildings;

but to preserve in tact [*sic*] all the original features of the park which are associated with the history of the place."

It was not that the government did not want to memorialize the sacred land, but that it was not in the business nor did it have the funds to do so. The prison site was of a different character, as it did not provide a field of battle for study or to commemorate the brave actions of the troops on both sides. As on battlefields, there had been a significant loss, but no one was a victor, and it could not be said that the men died valiantly defending a position or taking a stronghold. This was the story of the breakdown of humanity. Even into the twentieth century, passions ran high regarding the prison. Southerners claimed that they did all they could but were simply overwhelmed, and they quickly pointed out the deaths and terrible conditions in Northern prisons. Northerners pointed out the high percentage of deaths at Andersonville and that the men were treated worse than livestock. Both sides struggled to claim and control the story of the prison.

As requested by the quartermaster general, the site superintendents simply maintained the prison grounds and continued to improve the national cemetery and assist with burials. By the 1920s, most of the Civil War veterans were gone, and the efforts to memorialize the site dwindled. The WRC did place a few more monuments on the grounds and maintain the cottage, but little else was done to it. By the '30s, the bridges and many other structures put into place by the WRC and GAR needed repair, and the site needed more than just general maintenance. In 1934, taking advantage of the many programs created under President Franklin Roosevelt's New Deal, the superintendent put in a request for a Civilian Conservation Corps (CCC) camp. Major Duncan, the superintendent, asked for a crew to clear the woodlands, drain the swamp areas, replant trees, construct roads, renovate the star fort and work on constructing a museum. A few months later, the major received a reply informing him that only a few of the projects listed fell under the categories authorized by the CCC. Determined to have the work completed, Duncan resubmitted his request, and this time he outlined how each fell under the categories of flood prevention and soil erosion. In October 1934, CCC Camp 1411 arrived at army camp 3 to begin work at Andersonville Prison Park. The first order of work included cutting diseased and dead timber. When the crew finished, they built a curtain wall to further preserve Providence Springs and a road around the star fort, which included constructing an entrance gate and bridge. In the cemetery, the CCC built a trail from the flagpole to the north and south walls, with a turnaround at each end of the road, and repaired the bridges over the creek.

A HISTORY OF ANDERSONVILLE PRISON MONUMENTS

In the early twentieth century, Southerners made efforts to reclaim or reshape the history of the war and the South. There were a large number of monuments in the national cemetery and the prison park honoring the Union soldiers who had suffered in the prison. The GAR and WRC carefully protected the site in an attempt to ensure that the world understood the cruel way Southerners had treated the prisoners during the war. In 1908, the United Daughters of the Confederacy (UDC) erected a controversial monument to Confederate captain Henry Wirz in the town of Andersonville. It was the women's hope to bring to light what they believed were the correct facts of the prison and to exonerate Wirz of the deaths and suffering. A generation later, Southerners still felt that the prison park did not tell the Southern side of the story. During a Memorial Day speech in Americus, Georgia, in 1939, Nelson Shipp, the editor of the *Columbus Ledger-Enquirer*, suggested creating a peace park and memorial at Andersonville. Shipp argued, "The South has been done and is being done a grave injustice in connection with the cemetery-park as it now stands." The suggestion received strong support, and the following June, a group of businessmen from southern Georgia met to create the Andersonville Memorial Association with the idea of carrying out Shipp's suggestion. Ideas immediately abounded: one man suggested planting camellias and azaleas as a memorial to the soldiers buried there; the newspaper editor suggested erecting a memorial in order to "set forth the true facts relating to the Andersonville prison and standing as a lasting emblem of peace between the North and South."

The association enlisted the political assistance of Georgia congressman Stephen Pace to obtain permission from the army to use the land between the prison park and national cemetery for the peace garden. While the congressman lobbied to obtain permission and federal funds, Shipp toured around Georgia, giving presentations to the American Legion and Kiwanis Clubs, trying to garner support. The editor argued that the national cemetery was not a fitting memorial to the Union dead, but rather, it was a memorial to the hatred that existed at the close of the war. Shipp believed that the prisoners died because the South did not have enough food and medical supplies for them and because General Grant refused to continue the exchange. He told the clubs and the press, "The prisoners died as the price of northern victory. Why not give them credit for it rather than insinuating that they were killed by southern cruelty." The memorial association settled on creating a peace garden with a monument containing a chime tower in the center and plaques around the garden giving the true story of Andersonville to visitors.

Plans for the proposed peace memorial spread across the country in newspapers, and the superintendent of the national cemetery contacted the Woman's Relief Corps. The WRC rallied once again in protest to the peace garden. The organization objected, stating, "This would only serve to arouse sectional hatred and revive the bitterness of the civil war." In September 1939, the Assistant Quartermaster General Colonel John T. Harris supported the women's protest and told the organization that he did not want any part of the prison park given up to the so-called peace monument. He further added that he had no objection to a monument in that area if the government maintained it and any inscription on it were true to the records. Harris argued that it seemed to him "the inscription peace monument poor. [*sic*] Why not a monument to Americanism?" The few living Union veterans expressed their displeasure at the planned memorial. A veteran of the Sixteenth Connecticut wrote to the adjutant general and President Roosevelt that he would like to clean up the record just as much as any Southerner, but why restate things on plaques and memorials that were already espoused by Southern women on the Wirz monument? The writer further added that the state markers were not so radical, and they should remain to tell the real story. By 1941, due to the objections of the WRC and GAR and the looming world war, the memorial association dropped the plan.

Throughout the next twenty years, the army continued to maintain the prison park, honor those who were laid to rest and improve the cemetery. As the nation neared the centennial of the war, more people visited the prison park, and authors published popular books on the subject. The growing visitation and costs of maintenance led the army to request transferring the prison property to another government agency, suggesting the National Park Service. The cemetery superintendent argued that the War Department could not provide the proper interpretation required by the interested visitors. In 1958, Congress declined making it a national historic site. The quartermaster general continued to suggest the transfer of the property to another government agency. In 1965, Georgia state senator Jimmy Carter headed up a development and tourism committee in central Georgia. The group of community leaders proposed to create a tourism trail that would center on Andersonville. The "Andersonville Trail," as they named it, would connect Americus, Marshallville, Leslie and several other towns and tourist sites. A year after forming, the development group began pushing for the prison site to be named a national historic site and be transferred to the National Park Service. With political pressure from Georgia senator Richard B. Russell and the West Central Georgia Planning and Development Committee, the National Park Service completed a preliminary planning study to determine the viability of the site joining the department. The study recommended against accepting the prison park, arguing that the story was too negative and an extremely unpleasant part of the Civil War. The assessors argued that the park would have a depressing effect on visitors and that attendance would be limited to those with somewhat morbid appetites and those who had interest in the camp because of an ancestor. Finally the report stated:

> *There is a valid question however, as to whether many of the negative aspects of our history ought not be confined to written works and not given commemorative treatment. Clearly we would not wish to commemorate discreditable episodes such as carpetbag misrule, post civil war* [sic] *political corruptions in our larger cities and similar aberrations in our national life.*

A year later, National Park Service Assistant Director George B. Hartzog concurred with the report's suggestion and agreed that the site should remain under the direction of the army. The assistant director further added that interpretation would be difficult and would require careful, delicate treatment. The planning commission continued to press the park service to take control. In 1968, Georgia congressman Jack T. Brinkley joined the development committee and introduced a bill to Congress to create the historic site. The bill failed to pass due to the recommendations of the park service assistant director and protests from Georgians and the United Daughters of the Confederacy.

As word spread about the attempts to make the prison a national historic site, objections mounted against the proposed bill. The civil rights movement in the South created increased hostility toward the federal government and resurgence in the belief that the South was misunderstood and mistreated by the rest of the nation. Like in the early twentieth century, southerners, especially heritage groups, continued to try to control Civil War and Southern history. The UDC tried to stop the bill and get it repealed by arguing that nothing should be passed or done until it could be ensured that the southern voice would be incorporated into the interpretation. The president of the UDC argued that the federal government was attempting to distort the true memory and story of the South. One Georgia resident wrote to Congressman Brinkley protesting the bill, stating that government would only tell of the mistreatment of the Northern soldiers and that it

Georgia governor Jimmy Carter and Congresswoman Janet B. Scarborough Merrit looking over the bill to create Andersonville National Historic Site. *Photo courtesy of University of Georgia Libraries, Janet B. Scarborough Merritt Collection.*

was an attempt to cover up a similar story of Confederate mistreatment by Northerners.

Despite the protests, Congressman Brinkley and Congresswoman Janet Scarborough introduced a bill in 1969. Growing concerns of the Vietnam War and the hundreds of missing soldiers and prisoners of that war shaped the proposed park. Brinkley argued that the site would honor soldiers of both sides and would allow southerners to erect their own monuments. More importantly, the site would serve as a memorial to all American soldiers who have been held captive in the past and present. In the bill, Brinkley wrote that the new historic site would

> *provide an understanding of the overall prisoner of war story of the civil war* [sic], *to interpret the role of prisoner of war camps in history, and to communicate the sacrifice of Americans who lost their lives in such camps, and to preserve the monuments located therein.*

The new bill silenced some of the objections, and to prove that it stood as a memorial for all Americans, Brinkley, Jimmy Carter and a group of Georgians sponsored the creation of a monument to Georgia in the new historic site. To carry out the new park's mission, prisoner of war groups, veterans and the federal government built a museum on the site. The National Prisoner of War Museum would tell not only the story of Andersonville but also the universal story of American prisoners of war.

4

A STORY FOR THE AGES

It will no longer be said that the people of a free country do not fondly remember
those who have died that truth may live.
—Alonzo Abernathy of the Iowa Commission

By the late 1880s and early '90s, growing numbers of veterans, particularly Union veterans, began visiting the Southern battlefields. This allowed them to relive the times that haunted their memories and changed them forever. The need to tell their stories and what they believed was the true and correct history of the battlefield and honor those who bravely fought led to a preservation movement. This ultimately led to the creation of four national military parks: Shiloh, Vicksburg, Antietam and Chickamauga. Preserving the field of battle was not enough. Each state felt compelled to honor its soldiers through the erection of monuments, thus allowing its veterans to tell of their heroism and sacrifice.

Each state created a monument commission to memorialize its Civil War soldiers on the battlefields. Veterans lobbied for enabling legislation, and the governor of each state appointed the commissioners. Most commissions consisted of men who had served in the battle being commemorated. The commissioners, using funds allocated by the state government for the monument, held competitions or put out calls for designs. Granite companies and artists from around the country entered their proposals. After the committee decided on a plan, it worked with the granite companies or the artist to erect the monument and dedicate it on the battlefield. Most dedication ceremonies also provided the men a time of reunion. As the states rushed to place monuments on the battlefields, the veterans who survived at Andersonville began petitioning for the erection of monuments at Andersonville National Cemetery. It seemed only fitting that the states honor the men who struggled to survive and those who slumbered in the cemetery. Northern veterans believed that setting monuments at the site or in the national cemetery was a way to ensure that the true story of the prison was told and never forgotten.

This drive to tell the story of Andersonville coincided with a renaissance in American art. Inspired by Neoclassicism, artist and architects in the late nineteenth and early twentieth century began creating their designs in the Beaux-Arts style. During the mid-nineteenth century, American artists and writers moved to France to study art in the esteemed schools and saloons of Paris. The École des Beaux-Arts in Paris rivaled and even surpassed the Italian art schools. As a result, American art reflected the influence of this school. Those who could not travel to Europe studied under master sculptors who had. In 1882, America boasted thirty-nine arts schools, fourteen university art schools and fifteen different decorative societies. The new style of art placed emphasis on the body as art, like the Renaissance had done centuries earlier. Much of the artwork produced in the period focused on the human form and used allegory to make statements.

The growing movement in art and the growth of the granite industry provided veterans with a creative outlet to memorialize and tell their stories of the war. The allegorical nature and focus on human form allowed Andersonville survivors to vent their frustration and anger over the treatment and death of Union soldiers at the prison. The memorials told of Southern inhumanity and men refusing to dishonor their country and families by switching sides. In some cases, the veterans used the allegorical forms to place blame on the South and to admonish the future to never forget. The soldiers could express grief through allegorical figures of Columbia, angels and mourning soldiers. During the mid- and late twentieth century, veterans of other wars erected memorials to honor those held in captivity. The modern, realistic style no longer told the story of Southern cruelty and disagreement between the North and South but of the fear, sorrow, hope and despair of all soldiers who have been held captive during wartime.

NEW JERSEY

Here sleep the loyal and the brave,
By kindly death prison freed,
Who gave their precious lives to save
The Nation in its time of need.
—John E. Barrett of Pennsylvania

The state of New Jersey reacted quickly to calls to honor its sons who fell on Southern battlefields during the war. In 1896, the state erected the first monument at Chickamauga National Military Park—the country's first military park. After the WRC and GAR purchased the stockade grounds, the veterans in New Jersey began planning to honor their dead. These men would be the first to erect a monument at Andersonville.

On March 17, 1898, the New Jersey legislature appropriated $2,000 for a monument at Andersonville. The governor appointed two men to serve on the commission, and more than likely they were Civil War veterans. The men selected a large column design in Quincy granite. The top of the monument featured a soldier at parade rest gazing out over the graves of the brave. It is possible this was a stock design that the granite company offered the commission. The commissioners placed a time capsule in the sub-base for future generations to learn from. After careful consideration, the veterans placed copies of the New Jersey Laws, the Senate Journal and the House Minutes of 1898 and a copy of House Assembly Bill 188, an official list of the dead at Andersonville, a photograph of the monument, newspaper clippings about the memorial, a Grand Army of the Republic Union badge, a

The New Jersey state monument. *Photo courtesy of Hugh Peacock.*

The New Jersey soldier at parade rest overlooking the graves in the cemetery. *Photo courtesy of Hugh Peacock.*

bronze GAR horseshoe, a list of Medal of Honor winners, a list of the national officers of the Ex–Union Prisoners of War Association, New Jersey's ex–prisoner of war badge, a calendar from 1898, an American silk flag and a staff inside the box. Visiting groups and veterans found the monument inspiring and returned home to lobby for their own state memorials.

PENNSYLVANIA

Forever the monument will stand as silent reproach to the barbarianism that needlessly and wantonly took the lives of so many thousands of brave noble young Americans.
—Pennsylvania monument dedication

The sun shone brightly as the veterans milled about, admiring the stone pavilion and tasting the cool, refreshing water that poured from the fountain they had just dedicated. Many Pennsylvania members of the Ex–Union Prisoners of War Association recalled their first taste of the water back in 1864. After the dedication of Providence Springhouse, the veterans

The Pennsylvania state monument entrance.

visited the national cemetery to pay their respects to the men who never left. While walking among the long rows of white stones, they noticed a tall monument. The old men gathered around to admire the New Jersey monument and its granite soldier keeping a watchful eye over the graves. The men agreed that Pennsylvania should erect a memorial to honor their comrades who rested in the cemetery.

Returning to Pennsylvania, the group of men quickly contacted their local state representatives about introducing a bill to erect a memorial for those who suffered at Andersonville. The state had dedicated a monument at

A HISTORY OF ANDERSONVILLE PRISON MONUMENTS

Chickamauga National Military park, and a group of veterans were lobbying for a monument at Shiloh National Military Park, so it only seemed fitting that the state honor the 1,849 Pennsylvania soldiers who perished in the prison. Working to guarantee that the prisoners of war were not forgotten, the men contacted Governor William Stone. The governor, a former Union veteran, supported the idea, and in early October 1901, the Pennsylvania legislature passed a bill authorizing the erection of a monument at Andersonville. The state appropriated $25,000 for the task, and Stone approved the project but withheld the approval of the money due to insufficient funds. To show his continued support for the memorial, the governor went ahead and appointed a commission of five men. Three of the commissioners understood the prisoner of war experience as they had lived it during the war. Senator Ezra Ripple, William L. Ziegler and Congressman Harry White were appointed to the commission and had served with infantry regiments and been held captive. Two of the appointees, James Atwell and James D. Walker, had served with Knapp's independent Battery E during the war, and William H. Bricker had served with the Third Pennsylvania Cavalry.

The men wasted no time. They met on October 25, 1901, in Harrisburg, Pennsylvania, to organize and begin work. The group elected James Atwell, the commander of the Ex–Union Prisoners of War Association, president of the commission. Ezra H. Ripple, a former Union colonel and Andersonville prisoner, agreed to serve as the secretary and treasurer. Immediately, the committee sent out requests for design bids to make a decision about what type of memorial to erect. After much discussion, the committee members agreed that they would be able to make a better decision after they selected a spot in the cemetery for the monuments. The former prisoners took a train south to view the cemetery. After selecting the perfect spot, Bricker agreed to supervise the construction of the memorial and traveled to Chickamauga National Military Park to inspect monuments made of southern granite there.

The following April, the committee met again to decide on a monument design. Six monument companies made the final cut and were some of the largest monument and granite companies in the country. Among them was Miller and Clark Granite and Monumental Works of Americus, Georgia. This company was familiar with the prison site as it was only a few miles down the road. The commissioners spent three days reviewing each design before selecting one submitted by Miller and Clark. The chosen monument would rise thirty-five feet above the ground and be surmounted by a dome arcade. The barre granite memorial would feature two gothic entrances, which allowed visitors to enter and admire a bronze relief of prisoners getting water from Providence Springs.

Miller and Clark commissioned an artist to create the bronze figure on the top. The eight-foot bronze statue presented a prisoner of war "in appearance dejected and sad, facing forward and overlooking the cemetery as if looking in sorrow on the graves of the honored dead."

After choosing a design, the committee began working on compiling a list of the dead at Andersonville, writing the inscription and planning the dedication ceremony. As simple as it seemed, the men ran into troubles. On April 19, 1902, the men submitted their inscriptions to the secretary of war for approval and instead received suggestions for redoing it. The commissioners requested a list of the Andersonville dead from the

The Pennsylvania monument bronze of a prisoner. Notice the unshaven face, long hair and downcast eyes.

War Department and were told that it was not possible, as the department did not have anything but the original list provided by Captain Moore. After much searching, William Ziegler and James D. Walker reported to the commission that they were not able to compile a precise list of Pennsylvania's Andersonville dead. Between the many lists, there was too much variation. To add to their troubles, on April 22, 1902, commission president James Atwell died. The governor appointed James D. Walker, also president of the Ex–Union Prisoners of War Association, as the new president.

The spring of 1904 held the promise of positive developments. That March, the commission traveled to Georgia expecting to see a finished monument. Everything but the bronze figure stood finished. The angry commissioners contacted the company only to learn that the artist had taken ill. Pressing their need to complete the monument, the men requested another artist complete the figure. The company refused to replace the sculptor. That fall, the commission, finally seeing a completion date ahead, met to plan the dedication ceremony. After reviewing the finances, they realized that they did not have enough money. The men agreed that they would have to get the Pennsylvania legislature to appropriate more money

Pennsylvania delegates and a wife at the dedication of the Pennsylvania monument, circa 1905. *Photo courtesy of Pennsylvania State Archives.*

during the next session or postpone the ceremonies indefinitely. Walker took it on himself to lobby the legislature for more money and was able to secure $16,000 for the dedication and transportation.

On December 7, 1905, trains filled with elderly veterans pulled into the station at Andersonville, and the men gathered in carriages and buggies to travel the road many had once walked down to the national cemetery. Mary E. Myers of Gettysburg, whose brother had died at Andersonville, unveiled the monument. The Honorable John E. Barrett read a poem he had written in honor of the men's dedication and sacrifice. An estimated five thousand people attended the ceremonies; many local black and white citizens paid tribute to the men. The few remaining Andersonville survivors stood in the warm Georgia sun recalling their time as captives but feeling happy to be dedicating a memorial.

Oнio

No more the bugle calls the weary ones,
Sleep noble spirit in thy grave unknown,
We'll find you and know you among the good and true,
When a robe of white is given for the faded coat of blue.
—Poem in Ohio commission report

The white obelisk rose toward the sky as the men walked around it, stopping to read the inscription. The three former prisoners of war all agreed that the inscription "death before dishonor" was most appropriate. The men had traveled over eight thousand miles and held sixteen meetings in order to create this fitting memorial. In the nearby cemetery, 1,055 Ohio soldiers eternally rested after their suffering in the prison camp. They only hoped that the former prisoners and their families would find the monument and its simple inscriptions a fitting memorial.

On April 16, 1900, the Seventy-Fourth Assembly of the Ohio legislature passed House Bill 585. After careful consideration, the governor appointed a committee of three former Union prisoners of war to erect a memorial to the Ohio men who died at Andersonville. In July, the governor called the three appointees together to organize and begin carrying out their task. The four decided that D.S. Wilder would be the president of the commission and N.B. Mason would serve as the secretary. George F. Robison, the third member, agreed with the decisions.

The Ohio state monument.

Before selecting the best design for a memorial, the commissioners agreed that they had to find the appropriate site first. In August, Wilder and Mason traveled to Andersonville to look over the cemetery and prison park. Lizabeth Turner and the groundskeeper met the men at the park and walked over the grounds with them. After visiting the cemetery, the men returned to the prison site. The ground where the men struggled to live seemed like a fitting place to honor the captives. The two commissioners selected a site on the west side of the prison near the original north wall.

The Woman's Relief Corps approved of the site at its national convention and deeded the land to the state.

After returning home and getting the deed, the commissioners sent out circulars to eight states calling for bids and designs for the monument. At the following meeting, the men took little time to pick a monument. They unanimously agreed to the simple obelisk design submitted by Hughes Granite and Marble Company from Sandusky County, Ohio. For the Hughes Granite and Marble Company, this was a one of several Civil War monuments it would create. Carmi Sandford founded the company in 1880 and, four years later, added his brother in law, William E. Hughes, as a partner. Unfortunately, Carmi Sandford died in 1893, leaving Hughes to manage the business. The late nineteenth century proved a booming time for the company. By 1890, the company employed fifty-five master stonecutters, sculptors and engineers. It created Ohio state monuments for the Shiloh and Chickamauga military parks, and the simple designs seemed appropriate for the somber setting of Andersonville.

Delays in the designs and models of the United States and Ohio coat of arms added to the slow progress and frustrated the commissioners. The carvers worked carefully to carve in large lettering the simple words "death before dishonor." Disappointingly, delays in transportation and the erection at the park caused the commission to delay the dedication until December 18, 1901. The Ohio secretary of state, the commissioners and their families traveled by train to Georgia for the unveiling. When the flag was removed, the crowd stood in awe of the beautiful white monument. The commitment and sacrifice of Ohio's soldiers would be remembered and honored forever.

PROVIDENCE SPRINGS PAVILION

The prisoner's cry of thirst rang up to Heaven; God heard, and with thunder cleft the earth poured out his sweetest water gushing here.
—Providence Spring pavilion

Veterans cupped their hands under the cool running water and took a sip of it. It still tasted as wonderful as it had many years ago. The aged men, often traveling with their families and other veterans, lingered at the small spring bubbling up from the ground. Their minds recalled how pure and refreshing the water was on that day in August 1864. When all hope seemed lost and the

Providence Springs Pavilion, erected by the Woman's Relief Corps. This covers the spring that burst forth in August 1864 providing the captives with fresh water.

very thought of clean water seemed like an impossibility, the heavens opened, rain poured down and a great clap of thunder brought forth fresh water.

In August 1864, the number of prisoners swelled to thirty-three thousand captives, and the intense Georgia heat beat down on them. To add to their misery, the water in the creek that ran through the stockade no longer provided a safe source of drinking water. On August 9, a violent storm pelted the men with heavy rain, and thunder crashed overhead. The waters of the creek flowed over its banks, washing out the debris and any invalid captive in its way. Men gathered buckets and bowls to collect the rain, and many stripped naked to allow the pouring water to cleanse their bodies. As the sun burst through the clouds and the waters of the creek receded, clear, sparkling water bubbled up from the ground just inside the deadline on the western slope. As the word spread of the fresh water, men from all parts of the prison gathered around to get a sip of the life-giving elixir. Men gathered buckets and cups and placed them on poles to reach the water and avoid being shot for crossing the line. The prison police obtained permission to enter the deadline and create a diversion channel so that the captives could easily obtain the water. For many who were losing their faith and sinking into despair, this tiny spring offered them hope that an omnipotent force was looking after them in their darkest hours. The prisoners began calling the water source Providence Springs.

A visit to Andersonville Park was never complete without a visit to this spring. In their reminiscences, men wrote of the incident and the wonderful water. Locals in the area dismissed the stories of divine providence, arguing that the spring had always been there but had been covered up during the construction of the prison. The rains, as they believed, only opened it back up. The GAR and WRC recognized the significance of the site to the men, whether it was preexisting or not, and built a small wooden pavilion over the spring shortly after taking over the site in 1898. At its seventeenth convention in 1900, the Woman's Relief Corps voted to erect a more durable structure over the spring. The organization agreed to the suggestion of a marble pavilion with tile roof and flooring. A marble basin would be centered inside to highlight the spring, with inscriptions denoting the significance of the place. The GAR donated $200 for a marble bowl to catch the flowing water.

The women hired Miller and Clark Company from Americus, Georgia, to create the pavilion and the marble fountain. The company gave it the utmost priority and used Italian marble for the stunning fountain, which featured an eagle poised above a knapsack. Water flowed below the inscription, which was from Abraham Lincoln's second inaugural address, and out of the wings of a peace dove. The Ex–Union Prisoners of War Association, which assisted with the grounds improvement and the creation of the pavilion, placed

The fountain in Providence Spring Pavilion. The Woman's Relief Corps and the Ex–Union Prisoners of War Association funded the pavilion and fountain. *Photo courtesy of Hugh Peacock.*

Children visit Providence Springs, circa 1902. *Image courtesy of the Pennsylvania State Archives.*

an inscription on one side of the fountain, and the WRC and GAR placed another one on the opposite side. On Memorial Day, May 30, 1901, a large crowd of WRC, GAR, Ex–Union Prisoners of War Association members, veterans, family members and even locals gathered around the new pavilion to dedicate it to those men who once quenched their desperate thirst with the spring.

MASSACHUSETTS

They were heroes. They served Massachusetts, America, liberty, and humanity…
So long as patriotism is honored and liberty cherished among men,
for they are immortal.
—*Massachusetts lieutenant governor John L. Bates.*

"Thirty-seven years ago, I little thought that anything would or could happen that would tempt me, voluntarily, to step inside of the old dead line [*sic*] of Andersonville prison," said the gray-haired former prisoner of war Levi G. McKnight. Now he stood surrounded by dignitaries from his home state,

The Massachusetts state monument. Notice the "death before dishonor" inscription on the keystone

fellow veterans and former prisoners paying tribute to him and the thousands of others who were held captive there. With passion, he praised those men who, years ago, preferred death to dishonoring their country. He reminded the audience that the Union would not be intact without their determination and sacrifice. The speech was short but moving. One more speaker gave an even briefer speech, and the lieutenant governor presented the American flag to Lizabeth Turner to fly high with honor above the sacred ground.

One Massachusetts prisoner at Andersonville died for every five killed in battle. For every sixteen soldiers who died from battle, wounds or disease during the entire war, one Massachusetts prisoner died at Andersonville. The group of former prisoners of war mulled over these statistics during their annual meeting in 1899. Some members of the Ex–Union Prisoners of War Association had suffered and watched friends die at the infamous Southern prison camp. It was a unanimous decision to petition the Massachusetts legislation for a monument at the prison park. In 1900, six men—two of who were former Andersonville prisoners—presented the petition to the legislature. The bill passed with little opposition.

The governor, W. Murray Crane, appointed the men who presented the petition and the two former prisoners to the commission. On June 6, 1901, Crane called the men together to organize and plan the project. They agreed to divide into two groups, Charles G. Davis, Levi McKnight and Francis Curtis, who served at Andersonville, agreed to select the location and obtain the land title. Levi G. McKnight; Thaddeus H. Newcomb, a member of the Massachusetts congress; and Everett S. Horton agreed to solicit and select the design.

In November, Horton and Davis traveled to Georgia to view the prison park. After walking over the grounds and gazing out over the twenty-five or so wells still visible, the men selected a site that had meaning to them. The spot was just fifty feet east and fifty feet south of where commission member Francis Curtis and two of his fellow commission members held on to life during their captivity. The WRC sold the land to the commission for a nominal fee. The other three members spent days looking over monument designs but unanimously agreed on the simple design by the William A. Richards Granite Company from Quincy. The selected memorial would be made from Quincy granite and stand fourteen feet high. The state coat of arms would be prominent on the front, and the keystone face would have the defiant phrase "death before dishonor." The commission also elected to have stones with the abbreviation MASS sunk at the four corners of the lot, with another one placed at the northwest corner of the stockade.

On December 19, 1901, the lieutenant governor of Massachusetts, a large delegation of state dignitaries and officials and the commissioners stepped off the trains near the prison site. Carriages took them to the covered monument. As the dedication ceremony began, a freezing rain began to fall. Due to the weather, Lizabeth Turner unveiled the monument, made a few brief patriotic remarks and laid a wreath at the base of the memorial. The group then moved to the WRC cottage to finish the ceremony. At the close of the program, the delegation presented Turner with the flag so that it could fly over the sacred ground.

RHODE ISLAND

Let every brave man's death in this prison, let every monument here erected to his memory, be flagstones paving the way to universal peace.
—Rhode Island governor Lucius F.C. Garvin

It was not a long list of names in comparison to some states, but it had great meaning and created great sorrow for all who listened. Senator Edward L. Freeman presented the report listing the names of the seventy-four Rhode Island men who died at Andersonville prison during the Civil War. The representatives and veterans were angry and horrified at what had happened at Andersonville. Senator Freeman finished his presentation by submitting a resolution. He wanted to make sure that the people of Rhode Island would not forget and would forever honor these brave men.

On April 4, 1902, Senator Edward Freeman had little trouble getting a resolution passed to erect a memorial in Georgia. The legislature created a special joint committee consisting of members from the senate and the house. The governor appointed Senator Freeman and Henry Eldridge, and the speaker of the house added Walter Durfee, John C. Kenyon and Lucius F.C. Garvin. A few weeks later, the men met at the statehouse and elected Edward Freeman chairman and Walter Durfee secretary. To be more efficient in getting the work done, they created committees. Durfee and Kenyon would work on obtaining designs, Freeman would handle all the correspondence and Durfee would work on transportation.

After several meetings, the subcommittee responsible for the design made a presentation. Durfee and Kenyon, at their own expense, visited the Gettysburg battlefield to look at monuments there and then returned

The Rhode Island state monument. *Photo courtesy of NPS volunteer Ava Joiner.*

to decide on a design from those submitted. The men presented a simple granite design from A.G. Crumb and Son from Waverly, Rhode Island. Using the appropriated $6,500 from the legislature, the commission decided to use Waverly granite for the monument, place the state coat of arms in bronze on the front and inscribe the names of those men from Rhode Island who were held captive at the prison.

Crumb and Sons completed the monument without many problems, and Gorham Manufacturing of Rhode Island created the coat of arms and the thirteen bronze stars that represented the thirteen original states in time for the dedication ceremony set for Thursday, April 30, 1903. The commissioner, government officials and a few Civil War veterans left Providence on April 28 on the Federal Express to go to Andersonville, Georgia. After an evening stopover in Washington, D.C., the group arrived. Lizabeth Turner and some locals joined the group around the recently erected monument. Turner gave a short speech and then removed the flag covering the memorial. At the end of the ceremony, the group traveled through the cemetery, paying their respects to the men who gave their all for the Union cause.

MICHIGAN

Theirs was not the glory of death on the firing line…they were mustered out as a heritage to the nation and the memory of a devotion as limitless as eternity itself.
—*Michigan governor Aaron T. Bliss*

The elderly man walked slowly across the open field. The man, Dr. J.A. Griffin, stopped to gaze down at a hole dug deep into the ground. He lingered over the hole. The image from years ago when he was a youth standing on the same ground came flooding back to him. As Griffin looked into the former well, he could almost hear the chatter of the men who dug the well, smell the sewage and sweaty men and feel his ragged shoes on the red Georgia dirt and the sun beating down on his thin frame. The former soldier tried to block out the memory of the sounds and smells of the prison camp. Griffin glanced up across the field and remembered the tall wooden wall and the uninterested stares of the guards. The man's heart broke for the friends he had left in the nearby cemetery. A few other men who had also resided along the open field years ago walked the grounds deep in thought. As they strolled through the cemetery staring at the names on the long rows

The Michigan state monument.

of white headboards, Griffin and the other veterans resolved that the world should honor these men and all who had survived.

During the late nineteenth century, many former Andersonville captives from Michigan began to visit the prison. Dr. J.A. Griffin of Michigan visited the prison park after the WRC took charge of it. The doctor knew firsthand of the pain and suffering endured by so many as he had been held captive there during the war. In 1902, after a visit to the park, Griffin attended the annual Michigan GAR meeting and suggested putting together a committee to petition the state legislature for a memorial at the prison park. The former Union soldiers agreed it was an excellent idea. Griffin, along with E.S. Jameson and George W. Stone, all veterans, worked to send out petitions to each of the GAR posts in the state, requesting signatures to forward to their state representatives.

The veterans had no trouble getting their comrades to support the idea. Griffin and his committee took the signatures to the state legislature and pushed for an appropriations bill. The politicians of Michigan agreed that the men who held their allegiance in the face of such brutality should be honored and appropriated $6,000 for a memorial. Michigan governor

Aaron T. Bliss, a Civil War veteran, quickly appointed a commission to honor the seven hundred soldiers and sailors held captive at Andersonville. The governor appointed George W. Lansing, who had enlisted to serve in the war as a drummer boy at the age of fourteen, and E.S. Jameson to the commission. Griffin received an appointment, but the governor later dropped him. Bliss wanted a representative from the Woman's Relief Corps on the committee. The governor appointed Jennie Carpenter to serve, and because the two were from the same county, Griffin agreed to step down. Carpenter was the only woman to serve on a state Civil War monument commission at Andersonville.

Although the Michigan legislature unanimously passed the bill, it did not put in a provision giving the bill immediate effect. Wanting to get the memorial completed while the veterans were still living, Bliss met with the commission in August 1903 and began to advertise for designs. Oddly enough, the commission received plans from only three companies. The group, including Governor Bliss, met in September to examine the proposed plans and select the most fitting design. After much deliberation, the commission chose a stunning monument by the Lloyd Brothers of Toledo, Ohio. The monument company boasted being one of the ten largest in the nation, and its founder, Edward Lloyd, had begun his career as a stonecutter on the Eerie Canal in New York. The company's talented sculptor designed a monument that featured the image of a woman representing either Columbia or New York looking sorrowful and downcast and paying her respects by laying a laurel wreath of victory on the top of the memorial.

As the monument company began working on the memorial, the commission began planning the dedication exercises. The group met on March 23, 1904, in the executive's parlor in Lansing with representatives of the major railroad companies. The group decided that the best rate and routes would involve several railroad companies, and Pullman cars would be needed to transport the entire delegation. President E.S. Jameson took charge of advertising and arranging the program. The group agreed that the entire trip should take no more than six days and that the governor's wife, Mrs. A.T. Bliss, should have the honor of unveiling the monument.

On May 28, the train pulled out of Detroit with Governor Bliss, his wife and his military staff. The president of the state senate, the speaker of the state house of representatives and several elected representatives joined the commission in the special Pullman cars bound for Georgia. The group stopped in Nashville where the governor of Tennessee met the delegation and gave a tour of the city's points of interest. On arrival in Andersonville

Left: The figure of Columbia or Michigan bringing a laurel wreath of victory to the graves of the Michigan dead and a quill to record their names for posterity.

Below: The face of the Michigan figure in mourning over the dead at Andersonville.

on May 30, the group found six thousand local black citizens waiting to meet them, along with members of the local GAR posts. Two companies of U.S. Regulars detailed from Fort McPherson joined the group to maintain the peace. As the Michigan residents traveled through the national cemetery, they noticed that the women of the WRC had placed a flag on every one of the thirteen thousand graves, creating a "grand and imposing site [*sic*]."

On completing the Memorial Day exercises in the cemetery, the group traveled to the stockade and gathered around the veiled monument for their dedication ceremony. After hearing speeches from the commission president and the governor, the group applauded loudly for the key speaker, General James Kidd. The general had raised a troop of cavalry during the war that became most famous for the dashing young officer named George Armstrong Custer. Kidd, advocating reconciliation, told the crowd that the Yankees and the Rebels were no longer enemies. The Spanish-American War had ended all that, and now America was a unified country.

MAINE

The soldier well faced a cannon's mouth in time of battle is called a hero. Then why should not a soldier who faces death as those did who lay around us here in these thousands of graves be called heroes?
—Commissioner Colonel Levi M. Poor

The old veteran spoke in a clear, loud voice. He recounted the story of his and of his fellow captives' suffering at Andersonville Prison. The old soldier reminded the legislature that more than two hundred men from Maine had died there during the war. Maine had placed monuments on other battlefields recognizing the bravery and sacrifice of its fighting men. Why should those who made the sacrifice as prisoners of war, holding on to their last shreds of dignity and honor, be forgotten? As the elderly man sat down, the representatives dried their eyes and began to take a vote on honoring the dead at Andersonville.

Colonel Levi M. Poor spoke from the heart when he addressed the Maine legislature in 1903, requesting a bill be passed to provide funds to erect a memorial at Andersonville Prison Park. Poor served during the war in the Nineteenth Maine Regiment and was captured and held prisoner at Andersonville. After the war, the colonel watched as the state honored

The Maine state monument.

the men who fought on the battlefields with beautiful and dignified monuments. Maine did not forget those who died in battle. That story would be told for all ages. Poor, recalling the indignity and deaths at Andersonville, believed that the prisoners should not be forgotten. It was important to tell their stories for future generations just like those on the battlefields. The colonel approached an old schoolmate, veteran and state senator L.C. Morse, about introducing a bill to the state legislature to erect a monument. Morse gladly agreed, and in 1903, he introduced the bill. While presenting it to the committee on military affairs, "every eye dimmed with tears." The resolution passed with no opposition. The state of Maine appropriated $5,000 for a monument at Andersonville to "perpetuate the memory of our patriotic Maine soldiers who gave their lives while confined as a prisoner of war."

The following month, the governor appointed a committee to carry out the bill. Serving as the chair, Governor John Fremont Hill appointed two former prisoners of war to serve on the committee. Because L.C. Morse introduced the legislation and was also a veteran, the governor appointed him to the group; he also appointed Levi M. Poor, who had served ten months at the prison. Realizing that his duties as governor would conflict with the commission work, Hill appointed S.J. Walton to serve in his place. After the first meeting, the men agreed to visit Andersonville to select a location for the memorial. For Poor, the visit brought back painful memories and only made him more resolved to create a fitting memorial. While visiting the park, the men discovered that the prison grounds were stark, and very little remained of the actual prison. The stockade wall no longer stood, and Poor disliked the prison site. He described it as being "a desolate place, practically in the forest with the exception of a cleared land." The commission visited the national cemetery and found that the stone fence and government management provided them reassurance that their monument would be well maintained through the years.

On returning to Maine, the commissioners began soliciting design proposals. The three men noticed during their visit to the site that other state monuments were dedicated to those who died. The commissioners agreed that the Maine monument would be dedicated to all Maine soldiers, including those who survived, and they agreed on a design by C.E. Tayntor and Company from Hollowell, Maine. The selected memorial would be made from Maine granite and feature a thirty-six-foot shaft with an eight-foot, nine-inch soldier on the top. The soldier would have his weapon in rest on arms. More importantly, the soldier's head would be bowed in sorrow and respect over the rifle.

In the fall of 1904, as the commission finished up the last details of the dedication ceremony, it received pictures of the finished monument. On careful inspection of the photos, someone noticed that the right foot was placed forward. The veterans demanded that the monument company correct this mistake. On November 13, 1904, traveling by train, the commissioners and several members of the Executive Council of Maine

Left: The Maine sculpture of a soldier. Notice that the weapon is at parade rest on arms or reverse arms. This is a symbol of respect and mourning that was used by the military until sometime in the late nineteenth century.

Below: The face of the Maine soldier. Notice the downcast eyes and the look of sorrow.

and special guest Honorable Perham S. Heald arrived in Andersonville. A large crowd of black and white Georgia residents accompanied the Maine delegation to the cemetery for the dedication. Heald gave a speech to the crowd that spoke of the suffering and bravery of the men at Andersonville. In his speech, Poor reminded the crowd that the men who faced death in the prison camp were heroes as much as those who faced the mouth of a cannon.

IOWA

They fought their daily battles in silence, little dreaming that half a century afterwards the state they honored in death would here do them honor.
—Alonzo Abernathy

Iowa governor Albert Cummins felt strongly about honoring his state's Civil War veterans. These men had been willing to give their all to save the Union, and many willingly gave their lives on Southern battlefields. Iowa would spare no expense to honor its sons on the battlefield and at the site of the South's worst prisoner of war camp. Large, looming monuments

The front of the Iowa state monument. *Photo courtesy of the National Park Service.*

featuring wreaths, Fame, eagles and even a weeping Columbia would express just how proud and sorrowful the citizens of that state were over the war and their lost soldiers.

In the early twentieth century, the veterans in Iowa petitioned the state legislatures to appropriate funds to build memorials at Shiloh, Chickamauga, Vicksburg and Gettysburg. Realizing that the 215 Iowans buried at Andersonville had no memorial, the prison survivors lobbied for a monument as well. In 1905, the state legislature passed a bill providing $10,000 for a five-person committee to erect an appropriate memorial in Andersonville National Cemetery. Carefully reviewing the suggestions for commissioners, Governor Albert Cummins appointed five former prisoners of war to select the design and oversee its construction and to hold a dedication ceremony. That July, the group met to organize the commission and begin making plans. The commissioners elected James A. Brewer, who had served seven months in a military prison camp, as the president and selected Daniel C. Bishard, a member of the Eighth Iowa Cavalry and a prisoner at Andersonville for nine months, as secretary. The other men—Milton T. Russell, a member of the Fifty-first Indiana

"Compromise with the South," a political cartoon published in 1864 by Thomas Nast recommending against signing any agreements with the South. The figure of Columbia weeping over the grave of the Union soldiers inspired the figure for the Iowa monument. *Illustration courtesy of Billy Ireland Cartoon Collection, Ohio State University Library.*

and a prisoner for eighteen months; Martin V.B. Evan, a member of the Eighth Iowa Cavalry and a prisoner for eight months; and Winslow C. Tompkins, a member of the Twelfth U.S. Infantry and a prisoner for eight months—began working on finding appropriate designs and granite companies.

It was important that the monument convey the right message. The men traveled south to visit the camp and look at the designs used by other states for their memorials. Nothing they saw on their visit seemed to be the appropriate message or style. During a meeting, as the men discussed the message they wanted to convey and the type of memorial, someone remembered the figure of Columbia from a Thomas Nast cartoon. In 1864, Thomas Nast published a cartoon arguing that a compromise should not be made with the South or Union blood would have been spilled for nothing. The commission agreed that the image of Columbia weeping over the grave of the Union dead in the illustration was appropriate and the message they wanted to convey to all who visited the cemetery—the nation weeps over the tragedy at Andersonville and the war. Another member of the commission suggested a verse of scripture from the book of Revelations, "They shall hunger no more, neither thirst no more; neither shall the sun light on them, nor any heat. For the lamb which is in the midst of the throne shall feed them and shall them unto living fountains of water; and God shall wipe away all tears from their eyes." The same commissioner also suggested a line of scripture in honor of Providence Springs, "God smote the side hill and gave them drink." All the veterans agreed unanimously with the suggestions. After finalizing all their ideas, they hired Proudfoot and Bird of Des Moines, Iowa, to make their vision into granite.

On January 20, 1906, the monument stood prominently in the cemetery at Andersonville. The commissioners selected a spot that faced west and in a location so that all who passed through the cemetery would not miss the twenty-foot-high memorial. Iowa governor Albert Cummins made a grand tour of the South to dedicate all the Iowa monuments. The commissions for Vicksburg, Shiloh, Chickamauga and Andersonville traveled with the governor and other political dignitaries by train across the South. After dedicating the monuments at Vicksburg and Shiloh, the train headed across Alabama toward Georgia. On the morning of January 20, a day behind schedule, the train pulled into the station at Andersonville. The group disembarked and marched toward the cemetery. The Iowa Fifty-fifth band led the procession, playing solemn music while the first

Left: Columbia weeping over the Union prisoners at Andersonville. *Photo courtesy of Hugh Peacock.*

Below: A detail of Columbia's face on the Iowa monument.

A profile view of Iowa monument featuring a weeping Columbia. *Photo courtesy of the National Park Service.*

platoon of the Seventeenth U.S. Infantry from Fort McPherson marched closely behind. The governor and his staff led the way in front of the commissioners and the veterans, and visiting friends and local citizens marched in the rear. One commissioner remembered that the march to the cemetery was "a march that will never be forgotten by those who took part in it, so sad and mournful."

The group gathered around the impressive monument that tugged at the hearts of all who admired it. Captain J.A. Brewer, chairman of the Andersonville commission, presented the memorial to Governor Cummins. The governor made a speech in which he referred to the woman on the monument as "Iowa weeping, suffering and grieving over the sons she lost. She rests upon a column of enduring granite." Later that day, after the group toured the grounds, the band gave a concert on the prison park grounds near Providence Springs. Sad but happy to have acknowledged and paid tribute to the fallen sons of Iowa at Andersonville, the group boarded the train and headed north to Chickamauga.

WISCONSIN

They gave to the cause of human liberty the last full measure of devotion.
—Honorable Levi H. Bancroft of Wisconsin

Wisconsin contributed its fair share of soldiers during the war. The state fielded fifty-two regiments of infantry, four regiments of cavalry, thirteen batteries of light artillery and one full artillery battery. In all, the state sent almost 100,000 men to the battlefields in the South, and more than 12,000 of them gave their lives to save the Union. Of that staggering number, 378 of those men died at Andersonville Prison. It may seem like a small number compared to losses on the battlefield, but it was a tragic loss that many believed should not have happened.

By the early twentieth century, Wisconsin legislatures passed bills honoring their dedicated soldiers. Their bravery and sacrifice for the state and nation could not go unnoticed. In 1903, the Honorable David G. Williams introduced a bill requesting $10,000 to create a monument to honor those men who remained loyal to the Union in Andersonville Prison. To no one's surprise, the bill passed and gave Governor Robert Lafollette the authority to appoint three former military prisoners to the commission. The governor,

The Wisconsin state monument. *Photo courtesy of Hugh Peacock.*

fully believing in the importance of the task, appointed D.G. James of the Sixteenth Wisconsin Infantry, Charles H. Russell of the First Wisconsin Cavalry and Lansing Williams of the First Wisconsin Infantry. All three men had been held captive at Andersonville during the war and were passionate about honoring the men who died there.

The three men wasted no time in getting started. The veterans were advancing in age, and those who had survived the prison experience suffered from lingering effects that often shortened their lives. On September 7, 1904, the commissioners met in Madison, Wisconsin, and elected James president, Russell secretary and Williams treasurer. At the meeting, they decided that it would be best to visit the prison park and cemetery to decide on a location. In November, they toured the site and walked over the very ground they once longed to escape. The site of the wells brought back memories of their captivity and the indignity of being treated like penned animals. The long lines of white headboards in the cemetery only caused them more sorrow. After the tour, the three men agreed that the stockade grounds where the men fought for their lives everyday would be the best location for the monument and decided on the northwest corner of the stockade grounds.

After returning to Wisconsin, the commissioners reviewed the submitted design proposals. After days of deliberation, all three agreed that none of the proposals were right. Governor LaFollette joined the men in reviewing the designs but agreed with the commissioners that "none of those furnished was considered appropriate for the purpose." The veterans went back to the beginning and advertised for design proposals. After the submission deadline, the men gathered again to review the proposals and agreed on one design. They called in the governor and a college professor to confirm their choice.

With a selected design, they realized that they would need more money to erect the elaborate monument and hold a dedication ceremony. Governor LaFollette did not disappoint the ex–military prisoners and amended the bill to appropriate an additional $6,000. The only stipulation to the bill was that the monument had to be completed on or before May 21, 1907. The selected design made of Georgia granite rather than Wisconsin featured a bronze eagle with a wingspan of seven feet, four inches. On the west-facing end, the commission placed the state coat of arms and near the base included the words of Union general Ulysses S. Grant, "Let us have peace."

In the early morning light, nearly one hundred residents of Wisconsin, including the three commissioners, boarded a train headed to Andersonville, Georgia. The former prisoners could not wait to see the finished monument and were anxious for the rest of the group to see the memorial they created for the beloved sons. Two days later, the train pulled into the station at Andersonville, where local black and white residents greeted the veterans and escorted them to the prison park. A local African American choir opened the ceremonies with a beautiful hymn, and Judge Advocate Levi H. Bancroft said a prayer and then gave a speech. After the unveiling and a special song by the wife of one of the commissioners, the group finished the ceremony with everyone singing "America." Pleased with the monument, the commissioners and the group left. They knew that visitors would little doubt the respect they had for their soldiers and their desire for future peace.

CONNECTICUT

It was not in the heat and excitement of battle that these men gave up life. No cheer of victory roused them as their souls took flight, but in the loneliness of a multitude, with a comrade only by their side, within the enemy's lines and under a hostile flag, these sons of our beloved state passed to their great reward.
—*Robert Kellogg of Connecticut*

The Confederate guards walked with purpose through the prison camp. They stopped in front a makeshift tent and barked out George Q. Whitney's name. They gathered the prisoner and took him to the prison commander. The Rebels had a train locomotive breakdown and were unable to repair it. Before the war, Whitney had been a machinist. Desperately needing assistance, the Confederates urged the prisoner to fix the locomotive in exchange for a parole that would allow him outside the prison stockade. Whitney straightened up, looked the Rebel commander in the eye and told him that he could repair every part of the train, "but as for doing it for [you]," he added, "I'll see you in hell and then I won't."

Whitney and the five other former prisoners had been part of the three hundred members of the Sixteenth Connecticut held prisoner in Andersonville. Forty-five years later, they stood looking out across what had been the very land where they were confined. Earlier, the men had visited the spot where they had slept before entering the place called Andersonville Prison. While looking out over the field, Whitney and the men noticed Old Glory flying high above the land instead of the bars and stars that seemed to taunt them so long ago. Each took a long look at the flag, wiped the tears from their eyes and scattered out across the field to revisit the memories of long ago.

The Connecticut state monument.

These men were proud to have served their country and their state as members of the Sixteenth Connecticut Infantry, and now they were proud to be honoring all the Connecticut men who had remained loyal to the cause in the face of degradation. In January 1905, the state legislature passed a bill appropriating $6,000 for a monument at Andersonville, later it would add more money to the appropriation for the dedication ceremony. The state governor quickly appointed five members of the Sixteenth Connecticut to the commission. This regiment had more members held captive than any other regiment from the state. Frank W. Cheney, George Q. Whitney, George E. Denison, Norman L. Hope and Theron Upson all received appointments and all had been held captive in the prison. The five men, eager to remember those who died there, sent out requests for designs from the major monument and granite companies as well as artists. In July 1906, the commissioners selected a simple but powerful design by sculptor Bela Lyon Pratt.

Pratt was a notable figure in art circles at that time. He was currently serving as the head of the School of Museum of Fine Arts in Boston, Massachusetts, where he taught students and held exhibitions. The artist had

A clay model of the head of the Connecticut soldier boy. *Image taken from* Dedication of the Connecticut Monument at Andersonville Georgia.

recently completed a statue of Governor Jonathon Winthrop for New London, Connecticut, and had completed a sculpture of young soldiers to honor the young men who served in the Spanish-American War at St. Paul's School in Concord, New Hampshire. Commissioner Cheney and the other members visited with Pratt to discuss the type of monument they wanted to create for Andersonville. The veterans agreed that the work must represent a very young man in a Civil War uniform and have the expression of courage and heroism "that [is] developed in suffering, strong, modest and hopeful." When describing what they wanted, Cheney added that it must be a typical boy of the North "and his bearing that of one who has learned poise by endurance."

With these specifications in mind, Pratt went to work to create the most fitting sculpture for the Connecticut monument. By the end of the summer, the artist invited Cheney and the other members of the commission to view the final sculpture. Pratt had created an eight-foot-high "sandy-haired Yankee boy, disarmed and helpless awaiting his fate with calmness and resignation." The veterans instantly fell in love with the figure and believed that it indeed represent the soldiers who served during the war. With the sculpture accepted, the artist went about arranging the shipping of the bronze and making sure that the granite pedestal was ready for delivery to Georgia.

While the sculptor readied the bronze for shipment, the commission began working on setting up the dedication. The men set October 21, 1907, as the dedication date. The commission's secretary, Frederick W. Wakefield, obtained the names and addresses of every living Andersonville survivor from Connecticut and sent out invitations to the ceremony. While the commission was mailing out the two hundred invites, Pratt stressed over the shipment of the monument. On October 14, the artist received word that the railroad had delayed shipment of the statute. To add to his stress, the granite pedestal had shipped almost a month earlier and had still not arrived in Georgia. Originally, Pratt shipped the pedestal via a steamer. The steamship company informed the

The bronze Connecticut soldier boy by Bela Lyon Pratt. *Photo courtesy of Hugh Peacock.*

cemetery superintendent and the sculptor that it would not ship the granite, as it was not properly boxed. Some believed that the real reason the company refused to ship it was because it could not handle the weight. On September 16, the stone had reached Boston from Chelmsford, Massachusetts, and could not go farther because it was not skidded and because of the weight. The steamer company sent the stones back to the granite company. Finally, on October 20, Pratt received word that stone and the statue had arrived at Andersonville. Needing to pay bills, the sculptor prayed that the army would get the monument erected in time for the dedication ceremony so that he could receive payment soon.

Pratt traveled to Georgia to oversee the construction of the monument. On his arrival, the artist was frustrated to see that Clark Monumental Company, responsible for construction of the memorial, had not completed it. With only a few days before the dedication ceremony, Pratt began to panic. He discovered that only the foundation and few stones were in place and laborers had just removed the center stone from the railroad car. The sculptor wrote to his mother that seeing the lack of progress made him feel depressed. Through the hard work of the monument company and cemetery laborers, they moved the stone to the cemetery. It was just in time, as the dedication ceremonies were schedule for 2:30 p.m. the next day. The following morning, Pratt and the laborers worked right up until time for the ceremony trying to finish the memorial. By time the veterans arrived in the cemetery to see their monument, only the bronze statue was not in place. Pratt had the statute placed on a temporary pedestal for the ceremony and then stayed to watch the unveiling and dedication ceremony. The sculptor was delighted and agreed with the attendees that the Connecticut monument was the best one there and even added, "The other things are rotten." As soon as the ceremony ended, the laborers finished installing the bronze.

While Pratt and the Clark Monumental Company scrambled to construct the monument, the commissioners planned the dedication ceremony. Of the two hundred invitations mailed to the state veterans, only eighty-three were able to attend. On Monday, October 21, 1907, the train dubbed the Andersonville Special prepared to leave the station in New Haven, Connecticut, with 103 passengers. Wives and soldiers brought bouquets of flowers to see the men off on their journey and a physician traveled with the group to provide care for the survivors during the historical trip. The group stopped in New York and spent a day sightseeing around the city before heading farther south. On Wednesday,

Connecticut veterans in front of their memorial after the dedication ceremony. *Image taken from* Dedication of the Connecticut Monument at Andersonville, Georgia.

the train pulled into the Andersonville station. It had been forty-three years since the men had left this place, and many walked to the prison site on foot, "just as they did before." That night, the survivors sat around a campfire on the prison grounds provided by the cemetery superintendent. A quartet of black students from Spellman College performed for the men, and after the performance, the old soldiers reached back into their memories and retrieved the old war songs they had sung around the campfires so long ago. The following day, the group visited the cemetery to search for graves and relics. The superintendent decorated each of the Connecticut graves with a flag so that the men could easily locate their friends. Finally, the time and day came to dedicate the memorial. The daughters of the commissioners unveiled the soldier boy to the applause of the crowd. Then, the group quieted to hear Robert H. Kellogg, a former member of the Sixteenth Connecticut and a prisoner of war, speak. Kellogg concluded the ceremony by saying the attendees "did not feel that we are leaving him [the Connecticut soldier boy] alone in a hostile or indifferent country. He was in the midst of a great sleeping army, to which he belonged and which he would soon awake."

A HISTORY OF ANDERSONVILLE PRISON MONUMENTS

Indiana

It is relatively easy to die on the field of battle, but to linger in captivity, while awaiting the inevitable, though slow, visit of the "grim reaper" is so infinitely hard as to be deserving of a monument.
—*Colonel S.R. Jones of Indiana*

Indiana would not forget its sons who fought so valiantly on the battlefields in the South. As the government created the national military parks, the state appropriated funds and created commissions to erect monuments to its soldiers. Colonel C.C. Schreeder, an Indiana veteran who served in the war, made it his mission to honor the 702 Indiana residents who perished in the Southern prison camp at Andersonville. The state could not forget those men who, in the face of cruelty, remained loyal until the end.

At the turn of the century, Colonel C.C. Schreeder made a tour of the South. He visited the battlefields he once fought on and those he knew only as landmark battles from the war. As he made his way through Georgia, he made a stop at the Andersonville Prison Park and National Cemetery. The colonel's heart saddened on seeing the rows of white headstones. Schreeder walked around, admiring the monuments erected by New Jersey and Ohio. When the veteran returned home, he became determined that his home state should honor its sons at Andersonville as well. In 1903, while attending the annual GAR encampment, the colonel organized a movement to petition the Indiana legislature to erect a memorial. The GAR committee—made of ex-prisoners, except for Schreeder—felt passionate about erecting the monument. Two years later, while serving as a member of the lower house, the colonel presented a bill to appropriate $8,000 and a commission for a memorial to the Andersonville prisoners.

The time could not have been worse for Schreeder and the former prisoners' bill. That session, representatives brought forth several bills requesting funding for memorials. They were all similar in nature to the Andersonville bill. The legislature, feeling the pinch of a tight budget and the need to honor the state's wartime governor, Oliver P. Morton, who had done much to help the war and Reconstruction efforts, thought it was only right to recognize his leadership. Schreeder and his committee were not discouraged. The men went to the governor to request that he ask the legislature to pass a bill for a monument in his speech. In January 1907, Schreeder reintroduced the bill and asked for $10,000 and a commission. The bill first went to the military committee, of which Schreeder was the chair, and passed with slight opposition. It then

The Indiana state monument.

went on to the state senate, where it faced opposition, and was then referred to the finance committee. After some political maneuvering, the bill passed the committee and went before the senate again. In March 1907, the bill finally passed, and the governor signed it into law.

The task before the governor was to appoint the right men to the commission; it would not be easy. The treatment of prisoners and the deaths of so many impassioned the former Civil War veterans, whether they were prisoners or not. As soon as the news spread of the governor creating a commission to build a monument, the letters of recommendation and requests for appointment came flooding in. Most of the men seeking appointment were veterans, and most had been prisoners of war. Despite having initiated the idea and authoring the bill, Schreeder realized that he would have to politic to receive an appointment himself. As soon as the bill left the capitol for the governor's desk, Schreeder wrote to Governor J. Frank Hanly asking for an appointment. The applicant pointed out that he already spent several days at the prison site and was familiar with its ownership. Schreeder shrewdly pointed out that he had used his own funds to bring the issue to fruition. Two men wrote requesting that Hanly consider appointing John W. Vordermark of Fort Wayne as a commissioner. Vordermark was not only a man of wealth and culture but had also spent twelve months at Andersonville and was the secretary of the state Ex–Union Prisoners of War Association. Another letter recommended C.W. Digg as a commissioner. The writer noted that not only was Digg the writer's brother-in-law but also that he should receive the appointment for sentimental reasons. During the Battle of Chickamauga, Digg was captured by the enemy while trying to move a comrade from the field and was sent to Andersonville. A close friend

The Indiana commissioners at the dedication of the Indiana memorial. Governor J. Frank Hanly is in the center wearing a top hat. *Photo taken from* Report of the Unveiling and Dedication of Indiana Monument at Andersonville, Georgia.

Indiana governor J. Frank Hanly with Indiana veterans at the dedication ceremonies for the state memorial. *Photo taken from* Report of the Unveiling and Dedication of Indiana Monument at Andersonville, Georgia.

of Dr. R.C. Griffitt wrote to the governor recommending the doctor because of his time spent as a prisoner at Andersonville. In May 1907, after sorting through all the letters, the governor appointed Dr. R.C. Griffitt, D.C. Smith and C.W. Digg to the commission. At the first meeting, the men elected Griffitt president, Digg secretary and Smith treasurer.

Until the men visited the prison grounds, they could not decide on a monument design. After visiting the ghosts of their past in Georgia, the men selected a simple but elegant design by Montello Granite Company in Wisconsin. On completion of the monument, the commissioners, the governor, his staff, veterans from each of the Indiana units and former prisoners of war rode by rail to Georgia to dedicate the monument. On November 28, locals, both black and white, joined the citizens of Indiana to listen to the speeches given by former prisoners, the governor and a commissioner. The daughters of two veterans pulled the flag from the monument to the applause of the crowd. At the end of the day, the group returned to Indiana, feeling proud that they immortalized the men who preferred death before dishonor.

TURNER MONUMENT

And bending above them, through good and through ill,
The soul of the woman broods over them still.
— *"The Soul of a Woman" by WRC president Kate Sherwood*

On April 27, 1907, Lizabeth Turner, who had recently retired as the head of the Andersonville Committee and caretaker for the grounds, returned to visit the place that she loved. Turner strolled through the beautiful rose garden that she had so lovingly planted and gazed out over the monuments that she had helped to dedicate. The elderly woman loved her role in helping to perpetuate the

The Woman's Relief Corps medal on the Lizabeth Turner monument erected by the WRC after her death in honor of her work at Andersonville Prison Park.

memory of the Union soldiers at Andersonville. Later that day, she would leave the world to join the men she had carefully watched over.

At the 1907 annual convention, the women of the WRC voted to honor Turner's dedication and hard work with a monument on the prison grounds. The organization hired the reputable firm of Lloyd Brothers from Toledo, Ohio, to erect a simple monument that expressed their grief. The stone prominently featured the WRC badge and a mourning bunting carved in granite permanently draped over the top. On June 27, 1908, Turner's sisters in the Woman's Relief Corps gathered on the Andersonville grounds to dedicate the monument to the past president and caretaker. Her loving work would not be forgotten by the WRC, the veterans or later generations.

Wirz Monument

We have nothing there to refute the lies and slanders proclaimed in marble on all sides, nothing to bear witness to the truth, and to the brave testimony of Wirz and the men who died with him.
—United Daughters of the Confederacy

By the early twentieth century, Southerners began to try to justify the war and the role that they played in slavery. Heritage groups like the Sons of Confederate Veterans and the United Daughters of the Confederacy sought to immortalize the old South and the men they considered heroes of the war. The women faithfully preserved Confederate cemeteries, sometimes even relocating graves. The Confederate veterans, the United Daughters and the Ladies Aid Memorial Association raised funds to erect monuments to Southern leaders like Robert E. Lee and Stonewall Jackson in the former Confederate capital. Andersonville Prison, a subject of intense debate, evoked a rebuttal from Southerners. The South claimed that the deaths and inhumane treatment resulted from the lack of supplies and food in the South and that, had the North continued with the exchange system, the men would not have suffered and died. The former Rebels like to point out the deaths and conditions of Northern prison camps as well. By 1900, many Southerners were unhappy with the preservation and interpretation of Andersonville. As far the South was concerned, the monuments were prejudiced and did not give an even treatment of the story.

The monument to Captain Henry Wirz, Confederate commander of the prison stockade, erected by the United Daughters of the Confederacy. The monument is not located in the national cemetery or the prison stockade grounds, but in the town of Andersonville, due to the controversial nature of the memorial.

On January 12, 1906, the United Daughters of the Confederacy voted to erect a monument to the stockade commander, Captain Henry Wirz, whom the United States government had tried, convicted and hanged for war crimes. He was the only person to be tried and convicted of such crimes after the war. The women refused to believe or agree that Wirz was solely to blame for the lack of food, shelter and other necessities. The UDC, like many other former Rebel groups, argued that Wirz was merely following orders and making do with the resources he was given. Many in the South believed that the captain had become the scapegoat and took the fall for his superiors and Confederate politicians who really were to blame.

The location of the monument became a key issue for the women. Several monuments to Southern leaders and commanders were already erected or in the works in Richmond. It seemed only fitting to place the memorial there. The city of Richmond and the local UDC chapter rejected the monument, arguing that it would cheapen the other monuments. Henry Wirz's own daughter suggested placing the monument in Georgia near where her father had worked. The town of Andersonville, where Wirz's headquarters had been located, and the city of Americus vied for the memorial. Most agreed that Georgia was an appropriate location and that the monument would receive the most respect there. The UDC finally decided on Andersonville due to its proximity to the prison and the number of visitors.

As word spread in the North, the controversy over the monument grew. Understandably, veterans and former prisoners of war were outraged that the South would suggest honoring such a man. In February 1908, Union veterans gathered in Washington, D.C., to discuss how to stop the construction of the monument. The WRC, which had recently offered the prison grounds to the government, began lobbying to stop the memorial. The women of the South remained steadfast with their plan. Mary Young, the historian of the Savannah, Georgia chapter of the UDC, argued that the Northern monuments at Andersonville "inscribed a false presentation of Wirz," and it was the duty of the UDC to correct the injustice. As the Southern women decided on a design and inscription, they began a national fundraising campaign for the Wirz monument so that they could create a "lasting record of his murder under false charges."

The Union veterans and the WRC could not stop the Southern organization from erecting the monument. The memorial would stand in the town of Andersonville and not on the prison or cemetery grounds. On May 12, 1909, two trains brought people to Andersonville for the dedication of the Wirz monument. Due to the controversy, the Americus Light Infantry, which normally helped decorate Union graves, stood watch over the Southern monument through the night, protecting it from potential vandalism. The following morning, three thousand attendees watched Henry Wirz's daughter pull down the white bunting that covered the monument.

Then, a gun salute sounded. After the rousing speeches that exonerated the South and Wirz, the crowds went home. Some were happy that the South finally had a chance to tell its version of the story for future generations.

After the army took over the prison park, Northern states continued to erect monuments in the cemetery and at the prison site. Some had been in the works for years, and their commissions would not miss their opportunities to properly honor the men who faced death so honorably. The WRC, despite having given up control of the site, continued to furnish the cottage and erected a few more monuments.

The Woman's Relief Corps and Clara Barton

The women of the WRC were sad to give up the responsibility of caring for the prison site. They were dedicated to preserving the site and perpetuating the memory of the prisoners. Realizing that the government had far greater resources to care for and improve the grounds, the WRC handed over the Andersonville Park to the War Department. The superintendent of the cemetery, realizing how important the women were to the park, suggested that they erect a memorial to the organization. In 1910, at the twenty-eighth annual convention, the women voted to put a memorial commemorating the transfer to the U.S. government. The committee selected a tablet with a bronze sundial. The gnomon would be in the form of an American flag. This would allow the flag to reflect its protective shadow on to the dial. The words around the dial expressed the women's gratitude toward the men who served and sacrificed for the country. On May 11, 1911, along with the annual Memorial Day observance, the women dedicated their monument.

In 1914, two years after Clara Barton's death, the WRC decided it would be appropriate to honor her. Barton had traveled with the expedition to the cemetery in 1865 and helped publish the names of the dead. The WRC wanted to honor her accomplishments and inform visitors of her role in establishing the cemetery. The idea was to erect a simple granite, stone, boulder or bronze tablet. In December 1914, the women wrote to the superintendent requesting information about Barton's role in organizing the expedition and identifying the graves. This created some discomfort in the office. It was not clear how much Barton actually did in identifying the graves, and new research had shown that some of Atwater's records were incorrect.

Right: The Clara Barton monument erected by the Woman's Relief Corps in honor of Barton's work in identifying the dead at Andersonville and assisting families in locating their missing soldiers after the war.

Below: The Woman's Relief Corps monument erected in honor of its work preserving the prison site and to commemorate the transfer from the WRC to the United States. *Photo courtesy of Hugh Peacock.*

The army went back to the original reports and verified that Barton did not put together the expedition and had little role in the development of the cemetery. After receiving an answer from the quartermaster's department, Superintendent Bryant informed the women that in the reports, even Barton gives credit to Dorrence Atwater in identifying the graves. A memorial to Barton in the cemetery would not be appropriate but one on the stockade grounds would be acceptable. The courageous woman had spent her life helping the soldiers and their families during and after the war. Selecting a simple design featuring a red cross, the women dedicated the Barton monument on May 31, 1915.

ILLINOIS

Through this trial they passed with the same unwavering courage, the same unquestioning self-sacrifice, which knew but one response to the imperious call of duty, the response of service even unto death.
—Illinois governor Charles S. Deneen

The image of the children being directed to look at the rows of headstones captures visitors' attention as they walk in the national cemetery. The large, imposing Illinois monument beckons one to stay and examine the images carved and molded in stone and bronze. The men who commissioned the memorial hoped that all who entered the cemetery would hear their message, the lessons of Andersonville would not be forgotten and the horrors of it would not be repeated.

On January 29, 1907, an Illinois state representative stood before the general assembly and asked his fellow representatives to honor those men who died in the Andersonville Prison during the war. Many of the survivors were already passing away, and the state had erected monuments to its brave fighting men on the various battlefields. It was time to honor those who remained loyal through captivity. In May 1907, the legislature agreed and passed an act to "commemorate the heroism, valor and patriotic services" of the prisoners. The act provided $15,000 for the memorial and a five-person commission. Of the five appointees, three needed to be members of the Association of Ex–Prisoners of War of Illinois. In September 1908, Governor Charles S. Deneen appointed the commissioners; Lewis F. Lake, James Swales and Aaron H. McCracken were former prisoners of war.

The Illinois state monument, designed by artist Charles J. Mulligan. The artist titled the piece *Columbia with Youth and Maiden.*

The men met the following month and appointed Aaron H. McCracken of Chicago president, Gilbert J. George vice-president and Lewis F. Lake, a former prisoner of war, secretary and treasurer. In November, the group traveled to Georgia to select the best location for the memorial.

After some discussion, the commission agreed to advertise for sealed proposals and bids in newspapers in Boston, St. Louis, Chicago and Atlanta. In March 1909, the commissioners reviewed the submitted designs and selected a plan from Trigg Monument Company of Rockford, Illinois. Monument construction was such a lucrative business that it had become a competition between granite and monument companies. Shortly after the announcement, the governor received a letter from the Illinois chapter of the American Institute of Architects about the selected monument. A few days later, a committee of artists representing the different art societies of Chicago and the Illinois Chapter of Architects, also located in Chicago, went to the governor to discuss the accepted design. To be fair, the governor included representatives of monument companies, the commissioners and the designer of the proposed monument to hear the grievances. The three art representatives criticized the proposed design. After Commissioner McCracken talked on behalf of the commissioners, the artist committee left, and the governor conferred with these rest of the group. It was decided that the monument company would submit its proposed plan to William Zimmerman, the state architect. After reviewing the proposed design, Zimmerman agreed there were some flaws in the proposal.

The entire event inflamed commissioner James Swales. He wrote a letter to the *Rockford Star* newspaper, stating that there was no undue preference given in the selection process. The monument and stone were selected based on their merit and three of the five commissioners were prisoners at Andersonville. Swales, defending Rockford native Lewis Lake, told the readers that Lake was serving in the war before many of the so-called knockers from the Windy City were even born. Swales further defended the veteran commissioners by adding:

> *We think we know what we want better than some of our "pink tea" critics who stand for all that is beautiful in art, whether it is appropriate or not. We may not be critics as to granite, as the Fine Arts Society of Oak Park alleges, but we do claim to be experts enough to attend to our own business without the expert dictation of the aforesaid Fine Art Society of Oak Park.*

The governor entrusted the monument, design, sculpture and execution to Charles J. Mulligan, state architect Zimmerman and the Trigg Monument Company. Charles J. Mulligan was a well-known Chicago artist. The sculptor immigrated to Chicago from Ireland in 1885 and began his life in America working in the Pullman shops. Realizing his desire to be an artist, Mulligan enrolled in the Chicago Art Institute, where he studied under artist and professor Loredo Taft. His skills earned him the supervisory position over Taft's workshop, creating sculptures for the Chicago Worlds Fair in 1890. Afterward, Mulligan went to France to study at the École des Beaux-Arts. On returning to Illinois, he set up a studio and eventually began teaching with his former instructor at the school he had attended. Following the popular philosophy that urban areas should feature art for beauty and education, Mulligan worked with the Chicago Beautiful movement and created several public sculptures. The statues of Presidents William McKinley and Abraham Lincoln became some of his most prominent public works of art. The sculpture of the Three Sisters outside the Illinois Supreme Court became Mulligan's most famous piece.

Right: Columbia pointing to the graves of the Andersonville prisoners.

Below: The faces of Youth and Maiden representing future generations learning from Columbia of the tragedy at Andersonville.

Mulligan's Beaux-Arts and Neoclassical style helped him convey the story that the Illinois commissioners wished to tell. In June 1909, the artist presented his designs to the commission. The center pedestal featured a large bronze titled *Columbia with Youth and Maiden*. The sculpture's large Columbia outstretched her hand and directed future generations' attention to the graves of the men who gave their lives for their government. The boy and girl represented the future nation, which veterans hoped would remember the tragedy and never let it happen again.

Balancing the two ends, Mulligan designed two sculptures from the same Monticello stone as the rest of the monument. The two reclining figures represented the Union veterans in mourning over the tragedy of the prison. These two figures raised some concerns. On seeing the models, the superintendent sent a photograph and a note to the quartermaster general voicing his concerns. One figure donned a long beard and appeared to be rumpled while the other figure was neatly trimmed and dressed. The superintendent's concern was that it was an indirect way to represent North and South even though there were no letters or buttons to suggest this. He added that he was uncertain if that was the intent of the artist. Following up on this concern, the superintendent wrote to the commission requesting the artist to explain the figures. Mulligan explained that the sculptures were to represent the veterans of today; he had modeled them after men in the old soldier's home in Quincy, Illinois. The artist told the commissioners that he "wanted them to look somewhat as veterans of today, old soldiers who are doing homage to their comrades leaning on the wall ends in retrospective attitude." Mulligan admitted that he had considered making them represent the North and South, but after traveling through the South, he found no traces of hatred existing against the people of Illinois, and he now believed that the monument was a good way to demonstrate that they felt the same way. So instead of representing soldiers, his figures represented the veterans. In regards to the beards, Mulligan justified this representation by saying that he had "seen hundreds of our GAR men marching through the streets of Chicago of a type similar to the figures on the monument, and it was one of these men I intend to represent and not a confederate [*sic*] soldier."

Although the artist was meeting his deadlines, the granite company was running into difficulties obtaining the stone. In February 1910, Trigg Monument informed the commission that it could not have the pedestal piece ready until April 1, 1911. Horrified, the commissioners told the company that it must be completed by April 1910 and that they had hoped to dedicate the monument in May. Unfortunately, the granite company ran into more problems. The center die proved to be difficult to cut. Finally, in August 1911, the supervisor wrote that his company had completed the monument and would like payment. Excited, the commissioners traveled to Georgia to see the work. The monument did not meet their approval. The center die should have been one piece rather than two, the dowels were left out of the joints and the eagle was improperly fastened. The commissioners demanded the company correct the issues and told the company that they would not pay because the contract was not fulfilled. The Montello Granite Company, which had subcontracted with the Trigg Marble and Granite Company (Trigg had recently changed its name), informed the monument company that it was too difficult to cut one

Top: The sculpture of a Union veteran on the right-hand side of the Illinois monument. Some argued that this figure represented the South. The artist Charles Mulligan insisted he based it on veterans he had seen in parades and in the old soldiers home in Quincy, Illinois.

Right: The sculpture of a Union veteran on the left-hand side of the Illinois monument. The sculptor carved both figures from Montello granite.

stone to the size the commission wanted and that the quarry had been running poorly the last three months. The granite manager lamented that it was a shame that everyone was tied up on this one job because of such trivial matters and that they were going beyond their contract to get everything correct for the commissioners.

The following spring, the issue still was not resolved. In April 1912, the commission passed a resolution to have the center die changed to one piece and that the capstone and side slabs needed to be properly dovetailed. The monument company informed the veterans that to make the changes they would have to remake almost the entire monument. The Trigg Company representative recommended taking the monument down, shipping it back to them and surrendering any claim against the company. The representative noted that the expenses for the work were more than they were making for the project. Lastly, he informed the men that he knew of a party that wished to purchase a soldier's monument and this one would fit their needs. Trigg could have a different bronze cast for the pedestal. It would not be too hard to resell the monument without the bronze, and the company could recoup some of its losses. The commissioners refused to start over, so the monument company wrote to the cemetery superintendent requesting to remove the monument for corrections. The commissioners informed the captain to not allow the granite company to remove the monument. The company owner appealed again to the commissioners to move the monument for repairs. In their opinion, the contract was substantially fulfilled and to replace the monument would be a financial loss and a stain on their reputation. Threatening the commission and the state architect, who was overseeing the work and contract, the granite company informed the group that if it was not allowed to remove and fix the monument, the company would demand full payment of the contract.

The disagreement continued to intensify. In May 1912, the commissioners informed the monument company that it had failed to fulfill the contract and that the commission had the right to take ownership of the memorial and have it completed at the contractor's expense. The board of directors for the Montello Granite Company met and decided that Montello had fulfilled the contract and demanded payment from Trigg Marble, and if payment were not made in ten days, Montello would take steps to remove the monument. The monument company appealed to the commissioners, noting that it had the right to remove the monument if it was to be rebuilt. Trigg, the monument company manager, argued that the work could not be done on the grounds. This would require the cemetery to become a stone yard. The manager also pointed out to the commission that the Trigg Company had received nothing for the work and that the Montello Granite Company could claim and remove the memorial. This time, the veterans responded by issuing another contract requiring the monument be completed by October 1912 but still refused to pay until the memorial met their criteria. By mid-June, the commissioners agreed to remove the bronzes and waive all other defects if the center die and capstone were replaced. Trigg Monument agreed to the new contract but not without noting that if it were done, it was unclear if the state architect would approve of the work. Trigg contracted with the Clark Monument Company in Americus to do the job. Aware of the disagreements, the Clark Company reluctantly agreed to complete the project. Finally, in November 1912, Zimmerman and the commission accepted the monument and planned the dedication for December 20, 1912. Before a crowd of veterans and dignitaries, Illinois governor Charles S. Deneen dedicated the monument to Illinois' dead at Andersonville.

New York

Death comes with none of the inspirations that buoy the warriors in battle, no martial music, no thought of a fort to be captured or a height to be stormed. He meets death alone in prison, and in misery, with no dream of future glory.
—Honorable John F. Murtaugh of New York

The beautiful bronze relief on the back of the large, imposing monument tells the story of the prisoners. The haggard-faced man looks tired and shows signs of despair. The man with the upturned face eagerly hopes that he will survive and his country has not forgotten him. The front relief tells all who stop to admire the monument that the people of New York have not forgotten, and if they were able, they would place wreaths of mourning on the graves everyday. New York already had placed beautiful and impressive monuments on various battlefields, but the one at Andersonville truly expressed the sorrow and pain felt by the veterans, and the people of New York would make sure that coming generations would know that they mourned over the men at Andersonville for all of eternity.

New York was one of the first states to take immediate action after the war to place monuments on the newly created national military parks. In 1891, it formed the New York Monuments Commission, and former general

The New York state monument, front view.

Daniel Sickles headed up the group. The general had served at Gettysburg, where many of his men fell and he lost his leg. This, along with his other actions in the war, earned him the Congressional Medal of Honor. After the end of the war, Sickles was in command of the federal troops stationed in Americus, Georgia. This gave him firsthand knowledge of the atrocities committed at Andersonville. When the general learned that the WRC was making efforts to preserve the site and that the army had created a national cemetery, he pushed the commission to erect a monument at Andersonville in honor of the men who were held captive and died there.

In 1905, the New York legislature passed a law authorizing the monuments commission to erect a memorial in the national cemetery in Georgia. It also appropriated $25,000 to create a fitting memorial "to commemorate the heroism, sacrifices and patriotism of more than 9,000 New York soldiers…who were confined at Andersonville." The task of appointing a commission was not easy, as many veterans applied for the position. Five of the veterans who sent letters requesting appointments had been captives in the prison. Not limited to a certain number of commissioners, the New York governor appointed G.R. Brown, who had spent his sixteenth birthday in the prison; Robert B. McCully, another former prisoner; and Joseph Killgore, who had spent his seventeenth birthday in the prison. In all, the governor appointed fifteen men to serve on the commission. Most of these men were former Andersonville prisoners. Three were current senators, and four were assemblymen as well as veterans of the war.

The men wished to convey to all who passed through the cemetery the sense of mourning, the desire for peace and their feelings while imprisoned during the war. It would take the right artist to convey these ideas. The commissioners hired sculptors R. Hinton Perry and Louis A. Gudebrod. Perry had already developed a reputation with the monuments commission for conveying the sense of peace. The New York native began his formal training as an artist at the age of sixteen by enrolling in the Art Student's League in New York City. After three years of study, Perry moved to Paris to study at the Academie Delcluse, putting his emphasis on sculpture. In 1890, like many artists of the era, the aspiring sculptor received admission into the renowned École des Beaux-Arts in Paris. Perry had the honor of being the only American admitted that year. After six years of study in France, the young sculptor returned to New York and accepted a commission to create a bas-relief for the Library of Congress. One year later, he received a commission to create the *Court of Neptune* fountain in front of the library. His artistic ability earned him the contract for the Peace Monument at Chattanooga. In all, Perry would create more than thirty major pieces of art before his death in 1941.

Louis A. Gudebrod was a colleague of Perry and a former classmate. Perhaps the two men collaborated on the design for Andersonville. Gudebrod first studied sculpture and art in Paris as a young man. He returned to New York and enrolled in the Art Students League. It is likely that Perry and Gudebrod met each other while attending classes at the league school. Gudebrod, like many young artists of the era, received a commission to create a piece of artwork for the 1904 World's Fair in St. Louis, Missouri. Later, Tiffany and Company kept him in its employ to design artisanal lamps. His most famous piece, called the Nautilus, featured a mermaid sculpture holding a shell for the lampshade.

Working together, the two sculptors created a meaningful monument that combined realism with allegory. The Mount Airy granite monument featured two bronze alto reliefs. Perry created a nine-foot bronze relief on the front that featured a woman, possibly representing Columbia or New York, with her hand outstretched and holding a wreath. The artist wished to portray her decorating the graves of the New York soldiers. At her feet, in the foreground, he placed more wreaths so that she could finish the task. On the back, Gudebrod created a much more complicated scene that told a story. The artist wanted to show visitors the inside of the stockade. In the background, he placed the large wooden fence, and at the bottom, he prominently placed a young and an old prisoner from New York. Gudebrod turned the older prisoner's face downward, showing the man's weariness and disheartened state of mind. The other prisoner looked upward with hope. Above the two men, Gudebrod positioned an angel, bringing hope and holding a symbol of peace, coming to reassure the prisoners that the war would soon end and their troubles would be over.

The commissioners completed the task of creating and erecting an appropriate monument at Andersonville. By time the men paid for the $25,000 memorial, no funds were left for a dedication ceremony. The veterans would not travel to Georgia to dedicate their stunning monument until 1914, when the state legislature finally appropriated additional funds for the dedication. On April 29, 1914, with money available, the men planned a great event in the national cemetery. Wanting to make sure that all who had survived the prison were honored and saw the monument, the commission decided to send out invitations to the four hundred survivors living in New York. To attend, each veteran had to return a form stating what unit he served at the time of capture and confinement at Andersonville. The veteran also had to state that he "did not at any time take the oath of allegiance to the Southern Confederacy nor was in anyway disloyal to the union…and was honorably discharged" to attend. The list of attendees included 248 survivors. To further honor these men, Commissioner G.R. Brown worked on creating a badge to present to the survivors at the ceremony.

A bronze relief by artist Louise A. Gudebrod. The artist tried to represent the inside of the prison stockade. A young prisoner looks in hope at the angel bringing a laurel wreath while the older soldier hangs his head in despair. *Photo courtesy of Hugh Peacock.*

A close-up of the face of Gudebrod's older soldier on the New York monument. Notice the detail of the scraggly beard, long hair and sadness in the man's eyes.

On April 26, the train to Georgia readied to leave. By 1914, many of the survivors were advancing in age and were quite frail. Before the set date, some of the men died or became too ill to make the journey. Those attending had to forward the names of their physicians and obtain certificates from their doctors stating they were healthy enough to make the journey. It would be a grand pilgrimage to the South for the veterans and commissioners. Along the route, they stopped at national cemeteries and held services for the

Right: The image of a woman, possibly representing Columbia or New York, laying wreaths on the graves of the New York dead by R. Hinton Perry.

Below: A group of women, possibly the wives and daughter's of the New York commissioners, stand in front of the New York monument after the dedication ceremony in 1914. *Photo taken from* Dedication of the Monument Erected by the State of New York.

New Yorkers buried there. In Richmond, the group also celebrated Union general Ulysses S. Grant's birthday. On Wednesday, April 29, early in the morning, the train finally arrived in Andersonville. Carriages and buggies took the men to the cemetery where the monument stood draped with an American flag, and a platform awaited the dignitaries. This day was about the survivors, so only former prisoners were allowed to give the speeches. Even the clergy performing the benediction was an ex-prisoner. After the speeches, the drums rolled, and the flag was pulled away. The crowd applauded at the site of the beautiful monument.

At noon, the group traveled to the former stockade grounds. The state dignitaries gathered the veterans together and had them line up. As each man's name was called, he stepped out, and a badge of honor was pinned to his jacket by a mother, daughter, wife or granddaughter of the commissioners. The badge had each man's name, company and regiment. After receiving the medals, the commissioners hosted a barbeque on the grounds. It was the goal of the commission that "the survivors should have one square meal of local character upon the very spot where they once had hungered and thirsted for righteousness sake." After eating, the men scattered across the old stockade grounds searching for their old spots. At the end of the day, the men boarded the train to head back north. As they left, the state flags that they had planted on the graves of each New York soldier fluttered in the wind.

TENNESSEE

While it is substantial and somewhat inartistic yet it is characteristic of the rugged loyalty and patriotism of the men whose memory it is intended to perpetuate.
—*Tennessee state monument dedication*

These men had remained loyal to the Union despite their home state seceding. The war was a bloody struggle on the battlefield and off. Despite joining the Confederacy, Tennessee was a divided state. Most of the western portion of the state, cultivating cotton and owning slaves, supported the Southern cause. The mountainous eastern part of the state had many Union sympathizers, including the nation's vice president, Andrew Johnson. Many communities in east Tennessee fielded both Confederate and Union volunteer regiments. After the war, the state and veterans constructed memorials to the

The Tennessee state monument erected by the Tennessee Union Soldiers Andersonville Monument Association. *Photo courtesy of NPS volunteer Ava Joiner.*

Confederates. Everyone seemed to remember the honor and sacrifice of the battlefields, but few remembered those in the prison camps.

Union soldiers in east Tennessee created their own reunion groups. By 1910, in Knoxville, Tennessee, the survivors of Andersonville created their own group for the purpose of building a memorial to the 712 Tennesseans who perished at Andersonville prison. In 1910, Alexander Eckel, who had served with the Fourth Tennessee Cavalry, and John M. Harris and W.R. Carter, both of whom served with the First Tennessee Cavalry, met to create an organization dedicated to memorializing Tennesseans at Andersonville. Harris and Eckel were survivors of the camp and felt strongly that a monument needed to be erected at the prison park.

The three men created the Tennessee Union Soldiers Andersonville Monument Association and began enlisting the aid of fellow GAR members in Tennessee. The Woman's Relief Corps assisted the veterans with their fundraising by requesting that each of the women donate one dollar to the group. The veterans published appeals to their surviving comrades in newspapers and GAR publications. They placed advertisements and wrote articles requesting funds from the general public. The national WRC donated eighty-one dollars, and at the 1911 annual convention of the WRC, the women raised another twenty-five dollars.

By 1915, the men decided to end their fundraising campaign. Although they did not raise the funds needed, they did collect $866.75. This was not enough for the design they had originally proposed. The president of the group wrote to the granite company explaining, "Our friends did not respond to this patriotic enterprise as liberally [as they had hoped]." The men changed their design to meet their budget and selected a simple monument made from Tennessee granite. Alexander Eckel stated that even though it was not substantial or even artistic, it was "characteristic of the rugged loyalty and patriotism of the men whose memorial it is intended to perpetuate. It is made of the marble of their native state, as endurable as any marble that was ever mined from the earth." The lack of funds also forced the veterans to simplify their inscriptions. They simply put the word "Tennessee" on the base and on the front added "in memory" and the lines "we who live may for ourselves forget, but not for those who died." On November 12, 1914, a very small group of Union Tennessee veterans dedicated the simple but powerful memorial. It was not a grand monument, but it honored the Tennesseans.

MINNESOTA

*To them the roar of Cannon, the rattle of musketry amid the strife and din of
battle would have been solace and sweetest music.*
—*Commissioner Henry B. Dike's speech at the Minnesota dedication ceremony*

The mournful soldier keeps watch over the graves lined up around him. His
weapon rests in reverse arms as a sign of respect to the men who were loyal
to their nation even to the point of death. Sorrow and mourning was the

The Minnesota state monument by John K. Daniels.

message that the veterans of Minnesota hoped to convey to all who visited the cemetery. These men were looking for peace and reconciliation, not war or continued bitterness. The war was over, and now it was time to mourn and heal.

By 1915, the state of Minnesota had already erected monuments at the preserved battlefield parks. Two years earlier, the legislature had approved $25,000 for memorials. In 1915, the state's Civil War veterans pushed for memorials in the national cemeteries not located on battlefields and one at Andersonville. The legislatures approved a bill appropriating $10,000 for monuments at Arkansas, Memphis, Tennessee and Andersonville and also added the $6,402.77 unused from the earlier appropriation. The governor appointed a commission of Civil War veterans. C.C. Andrews of the Third Minnesota regiment, Thomas P. Wilson of the Fourth Minnesota Regiment, Henry B. Dike of the Fifth Minnesota Regiment, Levi Longfellow of the Sixth Minnesota Regiment and C.F. McDonald of the Ninth Minnesota Regiment all accepted the appointments and gathered together in Minneapolis on May 12, 1915.

At the first meeting, they elected C.C. Andrews as chairman and C.F. McDonald as secretary and put together an advertisement for bids. To get ideas for what type of memorial they wished to erect, the commissioners visited Lakewood and Oakland Cemeteries to look at monuments. On June 9, 1915, they met again to decide on the inscriptions and visited the studio of prominent sculptor John K. Daniels in St. Paul to look at the models. After some discussion, they selected a model of a private-rank soldier with his head bowed and bare and his musket in reverse arms. The statue would stand eight feet tall on a granite pedestal.

Daniels had already created several memorials. He was the designer for the Minnesota monument at Shiloh National Military Park and several other memorials in Minnesota. Daniels, an immigrant, was not old enough to have served in the war. Born in 1874, he immigrated to the United States with his family in 1884. While attending high school in St. Paul, Minnesota, the future artist received formal training as a sculptor. He later moved to Norway to study under artist Knut Okerberg. Daniels subsequently moved to Paris to study sculpture and, on completion of his studies abroad, moved back to Minnesota. After his return, he accepted numerous commissions for the state capitol. Daniels would create the monuments for Arkansas and Memphis too.

In September 1916, citizens around the state of Minnesota boarded trains headed south. The governor and adjutant general of the state joined the group.

They first traveled to Arkansas to dedicate the monument in the national cemetery there and then traveled to Memphis for ceremonies. The veterans, dignitaries and families then settled in for the journey to Georgia. On September 25, the group gathered around the memorial in the cemetery to honor the Minnesota dead at Andersonville. A local gentlemen who had served in the Twelfth Georgia Infantry during the war attended the ceremony. The commander of the Georgia division of the United Confederate Veterans, who was the speaker, called the gentleman up to give an impromptu speech to crowd. The old Confederate veteran spoke about the need for a reunion of the hearts and the country.

The bronze soldier on the Minnesota state monument. The soldier is portrayed holding his weapon in reverse arms, a nineteenth-century military display of respect and mourning. *Photo courtesy of Hugh Peacock.*

Eight State Monument and Memorial Day Proclamation

They fought for the Union, they died for the Union, and their ashes rest in the Union they saved.
—Woman's Relief Corps dedication ceremony

The Woman's Relief Corps continued to provide support for the prison park after it transferred the park to the War Department. The women continued to provided linens, furniture and other furnishing for the cottage and remained dedicated to assisting with the Memorial Day services at the national cemetery. The president of the WRC made a yearly pilgrimage to the

The Eight State Monument erected by the Woman's Relief Corps to honor the men from states that had not erected a monument in the park or cemetery.

park to check on the cottage and maintenance of the site. It was part of the organization's mission to preserve and honor the Union soldiers, and during the 1930s, the women erected two more monuments at the park.

In 1929, at the annual convention, the WRC decided to erect a monument in honor of Memorial Day and General John A. Logan. In 1868, General Logan, the head of the Grand Army of the Republic, declared May 30 as Memorial Day. This would be a day to honor all the fallen soldiers by decorating the graves and holding memorial services. The WRC assisted with observing this tradition by holding services in cemeteries around the country, most notably at Andersonville. In 1929, the women requested permission to erect a memorial in honor of Memorial Day. The monument, in the form of two tablets, carried the Gettysburg address on one side and the Memorial Day orders of General Logan on the other.

The Memorial Day monument would not be the last monument erected by the WRC. By 1934, it appeared that states were finished with creating memorials on the battlefields and Andersonville. The Civil War veterans were now gone, and memorials focused on those who fought during the First World War. The WRC realized that eight states still had not erected monuments in honor of their dead. In July 1934, the women wrote to the secretary of war requesting permission to erect a series of eight small markers to the states without a memorial in the national cemetery. This would be at no cost to the government. The markers would simply have the name of the state and the number of soldiers buried there. As the women began fundraising for their idea, they waited for an answer from the secretary of war. The response was slow, and the women requested assistance from the cemetery superintendent and from their local representatives. In 1936, after much consideration, the WRC decided that the best place and perhaps the easiest to get permission for would be the prison grounds. It also altered its plan and requested to erect one simple monument to the eight states lacking a memorial. This time, it received permission and dedicated its memorial later that year. Now almost all the states that had men die in captivity at Andersonville had a memorial.

Georgia

May we as Northerners and Southerners strike hands at the grave of our common brother, and know that the war which once divided us is over, and that we are forever united into one brotherhood, under one flag, one country, and one God.
—Minnesota Dedication ceremony

Although the Civil War had ended one hundred years earlier, there was still fear and anger among Southerners concerning the interpretation of Andersonville. Many Southerners felt that the South was unfairly blamed for the atrocities and deaths. The creation of Andersonville National Historic

The Georgia monument, by artist William Thompson. The monument honors all Georgia prisoners of war.

Site brought these feelings out in the open once again. The Georgia governor and state representatives suggested that site interpret not just the Northern Civil War experience but also the common experience of all prisoners of war. With veterans returning from Vietnam, many were realizing that all prisoners of war have common experiences, emotions and psychological trauma. Andersonville could honor Civil War prisoners, North and South; World War II prisoners and even Vietnam War prisoners.

To soothe Southern fears that the historic site would paint the South in a negative light, Jimmy Carter and the other sponsoring representatives suggested Southern states erect monuments. To create an example and to prove that the governor was serious, Carter proposed the erection of a Georgia state monument. On January 27, 1972, the governor appointed a study committee and asked representative Jack T. Brinkley to chair it. Carter wanted the monument to honor those Georgians who died in Northern prisoner of war camps as well as those who died in camps during the Spanish-American War, World War I, World War II, the Korean War and the Vietnam War. Congressman Brinkley reassured

Southerners that the Georgia committee would also make sure that the Southern perspective on the Civil War would be given through true facts and accurate statistics.

Governor Carter earmarked $110,000 for the monument project. The committee sent out requests for companies and artists to submit model concepts. After reviewing the entries and discussing what they wanted to convey, the committee selected a design by University of Georgia professor and sculptor William J. Thompson. Thompson, a Colorado native, served in the army in 1946. After completing his military service, Thompson enrolled at the Cranbrook Academy of Art in Michigan. In 1953, the artist completed his education and began working as a professor at Ohio State University and later, in 1964, joined the art department at the University of Georgia.

In 1973, American prisoners of war held in Vietnam began returning home. This momentous event influenced Thompson's idea for the sculpture. What struck the artist was the "solidarity, the courage, and the brotherhood they exhibited in their suffering to help not only themselves but each other to survive." The sculptor designed the piece to have no reference to any particular war or uniform, and he wanted the work to represent the idea of brotherhood and man's dependence on God. Thompson created a sculpture featuring three men marching in a broken line standing on a slight incline to represent the uphill struggle to survive the prison camps. The sculptor portrayed these men as having "exhausted their human resources and now look to beyond one another to God for their strength." The artist placed the two front figures with arms overlapping to emphasize the supportive nature of the group. Thompson wanted the piece to be open to interpretation but believed that the crippled figure represented suffering humanity that was beaten and near desperation and the central figure represented a Christ-like man who had accepted the other man's burdens and sufferings while supporting him. For the artist, the back figure could be interpreted in several ways. The figure could be blinded or a malaria victim near death and being led by the central figure. It could also be interpreted as the Angel of Death or release for the prisoner.

Influenced by artists such as Rodin, the sculptor created a one-third-scale model for the committee's approval. After the committee agreed that this was the interpretation and story it wanted to convey to all who visited the national cemetery, the artist created a full-scale model in his studio in Athens, Georgia. In August 1974, the committee traveled to Athens to give

Two figures from the Georgia monument. Thompson left the design open for interpretation but suggested that the center figure was a Christ-like man helping the other, which represented suffering humanity.

the sculpture final approval. The entire process of creating the piece took sixteen months, and the foundry took another six months for completion. On Memorial Day 1976, almost 1,500 people gathered in Andersonville National Cemetery for the ceremony. Governor Carter's mother, Lillian Carter, whose family resided not far from Andersonville and his daughter,

Right: The third figure Thompson suggested could represent Death, a blind man or a prisoner suffering from malaria and being assisted by the central figure.

Below: A close-up view of two faces from William Thompson's Georgia monument.

The Georgia monument, with artist William Thompson on far right, an unidentified woman in the center (possibly Thompson's wife) and a National Park Service employee. *Photo courtesy of the National Park Service.*

Amy, unveiled the only monument dedicated to soldiers from a southern state. It did not represent the Confederate soldiers, but all Georgia prisoners of war. Congressman Brinkley reminded the audience that they should remember the recent soldiers without question and those from Vietnam and their families should be given our deepest gratitude.

ODD FELLOWS OR UNKNOWN

No more the bugle calls the weary ones,
Sleep noble spirit in thy grave unknown.
We'll find you and know you among the good and true.
When a robe of white is given for the faded coat of blue.
—Poem from Ohio commission report

Being the superintendent of Andersonville National Historic Site can be challenging. There is the maintenance and responsibility of providing

The monument to the unknown dead in Andersonville Cemetery erected by the Independent Order of Oddfellows and Rebekahs. *Photo courtesy of National Park Service volunteer Ava Joiner.*

educational programming for the thousands of visitors who come each year. One of the important tasks is answering inquiries about the names of the dead in the national cemetery. Although Captain Moore and Dorrence Atwater identified almost thirteen thousand graves, time has proven that a few were incorrectly identified. There are still the several hundred that were never identified—the unknowns.

In 1983, the park superintendent finished answering a letter requesting information on a person's ancestor. The writer had evidence that their grandfather had been at Andersonville and died. The park service employee informed the writer that unfortunately there was no record of him in the cemetery, and he was probably among the unknown. One person wrote to the park requesting a memorial to the unknown be erected. The park superintendent sent a memo to the deputy regional director of the southeast regional office of the National Park Service asking whether such a memorial could be put up. The superintendent noted that over the past few years, over one hundred names have been identified as possible prisoners who died at the camp. He made two suggestions—either an interpretative plaque with the names or a formal monument, which was beyond the scope of the park's authority. The superintendent liked the idea of a monument to the unknown placed at the opposite end of the cemetery from the Georgia monument.

With no money or authority to erect a monument, the park superintendent looked for interested parties. The Georgia Department of Independent Order of Odd Fellows and Rebekahs agreed to underwrite a monument to the unknown soldiers in the cemetery. After reviewing the proposals from several local granite companies, the two organizations selected a simple design. The unknown would have a flat granite monument that sat eighteen inches from the ground in a blunt wedge. The memorial would be five feet long and eight inches wide at the narrow end and eighteen inches wide at the widest. On October 5, 1985, during the eighth annual pilgrimage to Andersonville National Cemetery, the Odd Fellows and Rebekahs dedicated the monument to the unknown. This was the twenty-second memorial erected at the site.

STALAG XVII-B

You know there is a saying
That sunshine follows rain,
And sure enough you'll realise
That joy will follow pain;
Let courage be your password
Make fortitude your guide,
And then instead of grousing
Remember those who died.
—*Poem scrawled on the wall of German prisoner of war camp*

By the 1980s, construction of large monuments had come to an end. There was no longer a need for monuments to the Civil War prisoners. America now turned its attention to the stories of those who had served in wars during the twentieth century. By the late twentieth century, the World War II veterans were advancing in age and their numbers were starting to decline. As the men passed away, the desire to commemorate and perpetuate their actions and sacrifices during the war increased.

In June 1988, the Andersonville park superintendent received a request to erect a large monument in the national cemetery. This was not to the Civil War soldiers. The request came from the commander of the American

The monument to the prisoners in Stalag XVII-B. Stalag XVII-B was a German prisoner of war camp that housed American airman between 1943 and 1945.

Former Prisoners of War Stalag XVII-B. The former World War II prisoners of war wished to honor all the men who served in the German prisoner of war camp XVII-B in Krem, Austria. Like the Civil War veterans, the World War II veterans created reunion groups that met regularly. Over one thousand former prisoners of war, wives, widows and descendants belonged to the American Former Prisoners of War Stalag IXVII-B. At the annual meeting in San Diego, several members suggested using the extra funds in their account to erect a monument to the prisoners of war in the European theater. Hubert Davis, a Georgia native and commander, suggested Andersonville as the appropriate place to erect the memorial. The park superintendent gave the request favorable recommendation.

The German government created Stalag XVII-B in October 1943, near the small town of Krem, Austria. The camp held prisoners from various Allied countries. For American airman shot down over Germany and Austria, this became their home until the end of the war. Crowded into long, poorly heated barracks, the men tried to survive the small rations of food and poor sanitation. Over 4,200 airmen would spend part of the war as a prisoner in the camp. In April 1945, Allied troops began closing in on the prison camps in Austria. The Germans forced the prisoners to march in the snow and cold 281 miles to Braunau, Austria, farther from the front lines. On May 3, 1945, the Thirteenth Armored Division entered the makeshift camp, bringing freedom to the captured American airman.

Hubert Davis—who became a prisoner in the camp after being shot down over Schweinfurt, Germany, in 1944—worked with the Clark Monument Company of Macon, Georgia, and the rest of the monument committee to create a simple but dignified memorial. The monument featured the seal for the ex–prisoners of war, Stalag XVII-B, a guard tower and barbed wire. Because the memorial was also to honor all prisoners of war held in Germany, the men added the seal for the American Ex–Prisoners of War Association and an eagle. The survivors of Stalag XVII-B held a reunion every year around the anniversary of their liberation; this seemed like the most logical time to dedicate the memorial. On May 3, 1989, the former World War II prisoners and their families gathered in back of the Andersonville National

The dedication of Stalag XVII-B. *Left to right*: Ray Elliott, commander of the Stalag XVII-B Ex–Prisoners of War Association; Kenneth Kurtenbach, Man of Confidence for the American prisoners during captivity at Stalag XVII-B; and Hubert Davis, a Stalag XVII-B former prisoner. *Photo courtesy of Bill Doubledee and Doris Livingstone.*

Cemetery, not far from the rostrum, in front of their monument. The band, color guard and other officials from Fort Benning, Georgia, helped former prisoner of war Hubert Davis dedicate the memorial. After special remarks

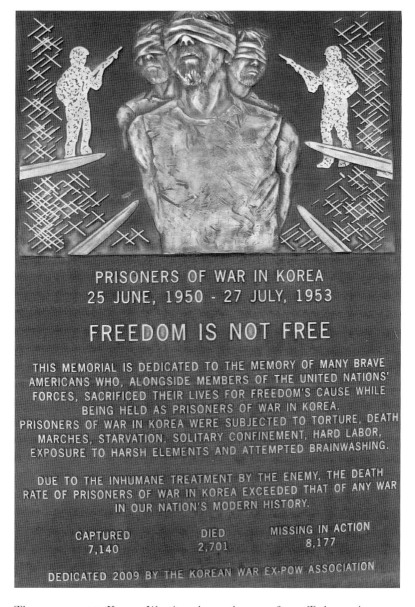

The monument to Korean War American prisoners of war. Today, various veteran organizations continue to erect memorials to military prisoners from more recent wars.

and music, Kenneth Kurtenbach, who had been the Man of Confidence, or the leader, of the American prisoners in the camp, unveiled the monument. After the ceremony, the men and their families lingered to admire the memorial and exchange stories of their survival in the cold, brutal German camp. By 2013, many of the men were too old and the numbers had dwindled to the point that the group no longer held reunions, but they kept photos of their memorial at Andersonville.

Although people still visited Andersonville to learn the story of Union prisoners of war, many people visited to learn about other American prisoners of war. More importantly, veterans from all wars began to make pilgrimages to the site, not to remember the men from the Civil War but to remember those from their conflict. The National Prisoner of War Museum at Andersonville National Park served as a gathering place for the former prisoners of war. Like the Civil War veterans, these men and women began to erect memorials. Although not as elaborate or as large as those of the Civil War era, the monuments still had meaning.

The prisoner of war memorial and courtyard at the National Prisoner of War museum. The memorial represents the shared experience of all military prisoners.

The prisoner figure from the prisoner of war memorial in the courtyard of the national Prisoner of War museum. *Photo courtesy of Hugh Peacock.*

Plans for the new museum called for a memorial to all American prisoners of war. The memorial contained a courtyard with a stream of water running through it and featured a brick wall with common prisoner of war experiences designed into the brick. In front of the image of the ragged, starving prisoners stands the bronze figure of a prisoner standing over the water holding out his hand with water dripping from it. The prisoner's face reflects the pain, torture and agony experienced by all prisoners of war. The artist hoped that visitors would take a moment to reflect on the experience of all military prisoners before passing it to see the grounds that once held forty thousand Americans captive on American soil.

EPILOGUE

Although the story of the American prisoner of war experience did not begin with the Civil War, Andersonville brought people's attention to these silent heroes. The treatment of prisoners during the war only added to the bitterness in the postwar years. Both sides tried to make sense of the numbers of dead and causalities and what happened in prisons and on the battlefields. As veterans began to remember the war, they wanted to tell their version of the story. This led to the desire to preserve the battlefields and erect monuments. Now the men could tell of the glory and horrors of war and the sacrifices made by the brave soldiers.

The story of the Civil War military prisoners does not fit this model. These men did not die charging the enemy line. Instead, they fought a silent battle that did not include cavalry charges and musket fire. The prisoners of war fought against their enemy by remaining loyal to their cause, despite the fear and feelings of being forgotten and abandoned by their own government. They remained loyal to the cause even when it appeared that death might overtake them. The daily struggle to survive in wretched conditions required the men to fight a battle within themselves. Prisoners fought to remain strong and refused to allow the enemy to break down their spirits and sense of humanity.

The feelings and attitudes toward military prisoners and their experiences are told through the monuments erected at the park. The veterans tell a different story in the monuments erected on the battlefields than at Andersonville. On the battlefields, the monuments tell of heroism, bravery and a noble death. This is often illustrated by the sculptures and reliefs of soldiers dying in battle while continuing to hold the flag high or by scenes of men rushing into battle. The sculptures of soldiers on battlefield monuments are usually at parade rest or holding weapons waiting to defend their cause. These figures show young, able-bodied men ready and willing to fight. Even the allegorical figures on the battlefields tell a different story. They often represent the states ready to defend the union or prominently feature allegorical figures of war. Often the statutes are holding laurel wreaths or simply represent victory.

The monuments at Andersonville tell a different story. This was the former prisoners' opportunity to tell the true story of the captivity experience. Even the simple sculptures of the soldiers are different from their battlefield counterparts. The representations of the soldiers at Andersonville are often skinny, tired and haggard looking. Instead of looking toward the din of battle, ready to fight, their heads are often hung low in sorrow and dejection. Even the clothes often represent the inhumane treatment by exhibiting the soldier in worn, tattered clothing, rather than crisp, new, full uniforms. The soldiers at Andersonville are not dying a glorious death, holding the colors high or even battle ready. The veterans chose to honor the dead by posing the statutes of the soldiers with their heads bowed and their weapons held in reverse arms, a symbol of mourning and respect. Allegorical figures at Andersonville do not represent goddesses of war or even of victory. The images of Columbia or the states educate and remind future generations of the tragedy. Often, she appears to be a visitor coming to pay her respects to the Union dead in the cemetery.

Even after 150 years, Americans are still trying to understand the tragedy of Andersonville and place blame. Despite the fact that we have fought several wars since and have had our prisoners of war treated in the most inhumane manner, we still struggle with the Civil War. Perhaps it is easier to rationalize the unjust and cruel treatment by foreign enemies because they are culturally not like us. Maybe Andersonville and other Civil War prisons are hard to understand because it was Americans inflicting the torture and treating other Americans no better than unwanted animals. Perhaps instead of arguing over who is to blame, we should ask how do we prevent man from losing his sense of humanity during war?

SELECTED BIBLIOGRAPHY

Primary Sources

Abernathy, Alonzo. *Dedication of the Monuments Erected by the State of Iowa*. Des Moines, IA: Emory English State Printing, 1908.

Andersonville Monument Commission, Illinois State Historical Library, Abraham Lincoln Presidential Library, Springfield, Illinois.

Andersonville Monument Dedication Commission. *Dedication of Monument Erected by the State of New York at Andersonville, Georgia 1914*. Albany, NY: J. B. Lyon Company, 1914.

Andersonville National Cemetery. Correspondence Quartermasters Department, 1934–1952. RG 92, National Archives and Records Administration, Washington, D.C.

———. Correspondence Quartermasters Department, 1936–1945. RG 92, National Archives and Records Administration, Washington, D.C.

———. RG 15, Box 35, National Archives and Records Administration, Washington, D.C.

Andersonville National Historic Site. Jack T. Brinkley Jr. Congressional Papers. Chattahoochee Valley Historical Collection, Columbus State University, Columbus, GA.

Averill, James P. *Andersonville Prison Park*. Atlanta, GA: Byrd Printing Co., 1920.

Beath, Robert B. *A History of the Grand Army of the Republic*. New York: Bryan, Taylor and Co., 1889.

SELECTED BIBLIOGRAPHY

Connecticut Andersonville Monument Commission. *Dedication of the Monument at Andersonville Georgia.* Hartford, CT: Lockwood and Brainard, 1908.

Dougherty, Michael. *Prison Diary of Michael Dougherty.* Bristol, PA: Charles A. Dougherty Printing, 1908.

Dragon's Tooth at Andersonville; or, the Lure of the Lost Cause, The. Johnson City, TN: William Hatch.

Elarton, J.W. *Andersonville Prison and National Cemetery, Andersonville, Georgia.* Aurora, NE: n.p., 1913.

Frank Hanly papers. Indiana State Archives, Indianapolis, Indiana.

Indiana Andersonville Monument Commission. *Report of the Unveiling and Dedication of Indiana Monument at Andersonville, Georgia.* Indianapolis, IN: William B. Buford, 1909.

Janet B. Scarborough Merritt Papers. University of Georgia Library, Athens, GA.

Kellogg, Robert H. *Life and Death in Rebel Prisons: Giving a Complete History of the Inhumane and Barbarous Treatment of Our Brave Soldiers by Rebel Authorities, Inflicting Terrible Suffering and Frightful Mortality Principally at Andersonville, GA and Florence, SC.* Hartford, CT: L. Stebins, 1865.

Massachusetts Commission. *Report of the Commission on the Andersonville Monument.* Boston, MA: Wright and Potter Printing Co. State Printers, 1902.

Michigan Andersonville Monument Commission. *Report of the Andersonville Monument Commission on the Erection of the Monument at Andersonville, Georgia.* Lansing, MI: Robert Smith Printing Co., 1905.

New York Monuments Commission. *Dedication of the Monument erected by the State of New York.* Albany, NY: J.B. Lyon Printers, 1916.

Ohio Andersonville Monument Commission. Rutherford B. Hayes Presidential Library, Freemont, OH.

Pierson, Hamilton W. "A Letter to Hon. Charles Sumner with Statements of Outrages Upon Freedmen in Georgia and an Account of My Expulsion from Andersonville, Georgia by the Ku Klux Klan." James Birney Collection, John Hopkins University Sheridan Library, 1870.

Poor, Levi M. *Report of the Maine Andersonville Monument Commission.* Augusta, ME: Kennebec Journal Print, 1904.

Rhode Island Commission. *Report of the Join Special Committee on the Erection of the Monument at Andersonville, Georgia.* Providence, RI: E.L. Freemont and Sons State Printer, 1903.

Richard B. Russell Jr. papers. University of Georgia Libraries, Athens, GA.

Russell, C.H. *Report of the Wisconsin Monument Commission Appointed to Erect a Monument at Andersonville, Georgia.* Madison, WI: Democratic Printing Company, 1911.

Samuel W. Pennypacker papers. MG 171.21. Pennsylvania State Archives.

Sherman, Ernest A. *Dedicating in Dixie.* Cedar Rapids, IA: Record Printing Co., 1907.

Styple, William B., ed. *The Andersonville Diary and Memoirs of Charles Hopkins.* Kearny, NJ: Belle Grove Publishing Co., 1988.

Voorhees, Alfred H. *Andersonville Diary of Alfred H. Voorhees, Co. H First New York Cavalry.* www.localhistory.morrisville.edu/sites/letters/diary.html.

Walker, James D. *Pennsylvania at Andersonville, Georgia: Ceremonies at the Dedication of the Memorial.* N.p.: C.E. Aughinbaugh, 1909.

Wilder, D.S. *Report of the Ohio Andersonville Monument Commission.* Clyde: Ohio Andersonville Monument Commission, 1902.

Wisconsin Monument Commission. *Report of the Wisconsin Monument Commission Appointed to Erect a Monument at Andersonville, Georgia With Other Interesting Matter Pertaining to the Prison.* Madison, WI: Democratic Printing, 1911.

Woman's Relief Corps. *Journal of the Nineteenth Convention of the Woman's Relief Corps.* Boston: E.B. Stillings and Co., 1901.

————. *Journal of the Twenty-ninth Convention of the Woman's Relief Corps.* Boston: E.B. Stillings and Co., 1911.

SECONDARY SOURCES

Bearess, Edwin C. *Andersonville National Historic Site: Historic Resource Study and Historical Base Map.* Washington, D.C.: Office of History and Historic Architecture, 1970.

Bela Lyon Pratt Historical Society. "Bela Lyon Pratt: American Sculptor." www.belalyonpratt.com.

Burnett, Bill. *Andersonville Monuments Andersonville National Historic Site.* N.p., 2000.

Burnett, William G. *Our Lizabeth.* N.p.: W.G. Burnett, 1991.

Cloyd, Benjamin G. *Haunted by Atrocity Civil War Prisons in American Memory.* Baton Rouge: Louisiana State University Press, 2010.

Davis, Robert Scott. *Andersonville Civil War Prison.* Charleston, SC: The History Press, 2010.

Faust, Drew Gilpin. *This Republic of Suffering: Death and the American Civil War.* New York: Vintage Civil War, 2008.

Futch, Ovid. *History of Andersonville Prison, Revised Edition.* Gainesville: University of Florida Press, 2011.

SELECTED BIBLIOGRAPHY

Janney, Caroline E. *Remembering the Civil War: Reunion and the Limits of Reconciliation*. Chapel Hill: University of North Carolina, 2013.

Lowe, William C. "A Grand and Patriotic Pilgrimage: The Iowa Civil War Monuments Dedication Tour of 1906." *Annals of Iowa* 69, no. 1 (Winter 2010): 1–50.

Marvel, William. *Andersonville: The Last Depot*. Chapel Hill: University of North Carolina Press, 1994.

Oates, Stephen B. *A Woman of Valor: Clara Barton and the Civil War*. New York: The Free Press, 1994.

Peterson, William J. "Iowa at Andersonville." *Palimpsest* 23: 209–88.

Poppenheim, Mary B. *The History of the United Daughters of the Confederacy*. Richmond, VA: Garrett and Massie, Inc., 1925.

Reaves, Stacy. *A History and Guide to the Monuments of Chickamauga National Military Park*. Charleston, SC: The History Press, 2013.

———. *A History and Guide to the Monuments of Shiloh National Military Park*. Charleston, SC: The History Press, 2012.

Rhulman, Fred R. *Captain Henry Wirz and Andersonville Prison: A Reappraisal*. Knoxville: University of Tennessee Press, 2006.

Sandusky County. *The Sandusky County Scrapbook*. http://www.sandusky-county-scrapbook.net/default.htm.

Savage, Kirk. *Standing Soldiers, Kneeling Slaves: Race, War and Monuments in Nineteenth Century America*. Princeton, NJ: Princeton University, 1979.

Speer, Lonnie R. *Portals to Hell: Military Prisons of the Civil War*. Mechanicsburg, PA: Stackpole Books, 1997.

Steinhorst, Stephanie, and Chris Barr. *The Prison Camps at Andersonville*. N.p.: Eastern National, 2014.

INDEX

INDEX

ABOUT THE AUTHOR

Stacy Reaves is an adjunct professor of history and geography at Tulsa Community College in Tulsa, Oklahoma. She is the author of *A History and Guide to the Monuments of Shiloh National Park* and *A History and Guide to the Monuments of Chickamauga National Park* by The History Press. Reaves has a BS in historic preservation from Southeast Missouri State University and a PhD in United States military history from Oklahoma State University. She has worked as a seasonal interpretative ranger with the National Park Service at Shiloh National Military Park and Fort Larned National Historic Site. Reaves has also worked as a museum curator for the United States Army and the Sapulpa Historical Society in Oklahoma. She has been the executive director of the Sand Springs Historical and Cultural Museum and recently consulted on the creation of the Military History Museum in Broken Arrow, Oklahoma.